* g...um*

Baba

Life, Teachings, and Parables—
A Spiritual Biography of
Baba Prakashananda

---

by

T I T U S   F O S T E R

North Atlantic Books
Berkeley, California

Essene Vision Books
Patagonia, Arizona

Agaram Bagaram Baba
Life, Teachings, and Parables—
A Spiritual Biography of Baba Prakashananda

Published by
North Atlantic Books
P.O. Box 12327
Berkeley, California 94712
and
Essene Vision Books
P.O. Box 1080
Patagonia, Arizona 85624

http://www.chiron-h.com/tol

Cover and book design: Suzanne Stasa and Bob Warden
Photos: Myriam Lanvin, Adrian Halpern, and others
Managing Editor: Bob Warden
Editor: Suzanne Stasa

Printed in the United States of America
First Printing 1999

Agaram Bagaram Baba: Life, Teachings, and Parables—A Spiritual Biography of Baba Prakashananda is sponsored by the Society for the Study of Native Arts and Sciences, a nonprofit educational corporation whose goals are to develop an educational and cross-cultural perspective linking various scientific, social, and artistic fields; to nurture a holistic view of arts, sciences, humanities, and healing; and to publish and distribute literature on the relationship of mind, body, and nature.

Library of Congress Cataloging-in-Publication Data

Agaram bagaram baba: life, teachings, and parables—
a spiritual biography of baba prakashananda / Titus Foster.
p.   cm.
Includes index.
ISBN 1-55643-287-9 (alk. paper)
1. Prakashananda, Swami. 2. Hindus—India—Biography. I. Title.
BL 1175.P7165F67 1998
294.5'092—dc21
[B]   98-17765
                                                                      CIP

*In honor of the Supreme Principle
who illumines both teacher and disciple.*

Contents

Acknowledgments

I would like to acknowledge and thank those people who so selflessly and unstintingly helped by donating their time, suggestions, love, and patience in making this book possible: Michael Mauger, Pierre Pulling, Michael Eccles, Philip Davies, and especially, Carol Williams and Gabriel Cousens, M.D. Also, my thanks to Kirin Narayan for the use of transcripts of audiocassettes, and to my wife, Pippa, whose encouragement is always an inspiration. Finally, thanks to Suzanne Stasa and Bob Warden.

Foreword

My first experience of Swami Prakashananda was in 1977 at Swami Muktananda's ashram in Ganeshpuri, India. He was a spectacularly fascinating-looking human being. His clothes appeared plain and simple in contrast to the richness of his Divine depth. His eyes were magnified by his thick glasses into beams of light. A subtle light appeared to be streaming off his round, succulent body as he seemed to almost float over the ground. I did not know what his name was, but it was obvious to me he was a holy man. There were a few people walking with him and I was so attracted by this radiant being that I just began to walk along also. After a while the small group settled around him in an informal way on a porch. I could not get over how radiant his body appeared. It actually seemed to glow. As he talked and shared the most engaging stories through a translator, his presence filled the room with a simple, all-encompassing love. I felt I was in the presence of the Divine mother. My being felt as if it were in a womb of love. My whole organism felt nourished in a uniquely total way. This spiritual feast went on for hours. So began my relationship with the great being called Swami Prakashananda Saraswati. It would be an understatement to say I was inspired.

Over the years, I had opportunities to spend more time with him. He was an ardent devotee of the Divine Mother and the love that emanated from him only hinted at the degree to which he had merged with the Goddess and become the Divine Mother disguised in the form of a man.

In the background was his devotion to Dattatreya, an incarnation combining Shiva, Vishnu, and Brahma, who is the primordial embodiment of the Guru Principle. His devotion to Dattatreya was so great that a tree trunk with three separate trees growing out of it (symbolizing the three aspects of Dattatreya) even grew in his Sapta Shringh ashram. A small temple to Dattatreya was built by Prakashananda in honor of this special tree.

Swami Prakashananda, although often appearing to worship an external form, lived in the conscious awareness of a jnani. A jnani is one whose awareness goes beyond the illusion of all form (however Divine), spiritual visions, and even the highly esteemed vision of the Blue Pearl. Swami Prakashananda was established in the noncausal joy of the nondual awareness of the "great nothingness." It was this profound level of consciousness that gave spiritual power to Swami Prakashananda's mystical simplicity, his overwhelming radiation of love, and his immunity to the attractions of power, money, and sex. He was directly experiencing and expressing the eternal, divine wealth of God.

Although he fiercely followed his own teaching of the inner Guru as the ultimate guru, the third part of his spiritual background came from his love of his physical guru, Swami Muktananda.

He often jokingly referred to himself as an "agaram bagaram" (hodgepodge) swami. The sound of these words, like many of his humorous yet pointed stories, is quite descriptive of how his life was lived. Prakashananda was free from worldly entanglements, yet played fully and humorously in the world in his own independent, iconoclastic way. In the Jewish tradition, he would be compared to a hidden Tzaddik. He refused to take the position of a guru, yet served as a "guru uncle," or what I would call a spiritual mentor, to thousands of spiritually hungry humans ranging from indigenous Indian children to sophisticated Western professionals. He was the respected guru uncle to many Indian holy men and sadhus in Maharashtra state.

After leaving Sapta Shringh moutain where he had lived for 27 years in a 9' x 9' x 9' room, Swami Prakashananda led a physically and socially simple life in a humble two-room dwelling where a devotee invited him to live in Nasik. As an "agaram bagaram" swami, he consistently remained immune to the temptations of power, riches, and sex that seem to infect and bring down so many present-day spiritual teachers. Prakashananda shared almost all of what was offered to him with the financially poor children and adults who visited his ashram.

Unencumbered by large organizations and worldly temptations, he was free to express the play of the inner Divine light which shone so radiantly through every aspect of his life. It led him to feed the God in everyone, both physically and spiritually. This manifested in a program which cared for the financially disadvantaged children in the Sapta Shringh area. The children who lived in his humble ashram, along with many of the children of the area, were fed on a daily basis. This program has been active more than thirty years.

He was the embodiment of what he taught. The guru exists within you. Follow this inner direction and do not get stuck in the enmeshment of spiritual organizations, spiritual formulas, or belief systems that do not always encourage and allow a person to follow the inner guidance of the Guru Tattva, the formless, inner guru. The noncausal joy of the inner guru always seemed to bubble through him with a mischievous, humorous radiance that would spontaneously evoke the heart to smile.

Although liberated, he maintained a continual spiritual vigilance. Near the end of my time with him, Prakashananda graced me with one whole day alone with him and his translator, traveling around Bombay. As we experienced the shakti manifesting as the myriad faces of humanity in the city, he compassionately explained to me the subtleties of liberation and the necessity of maintaining spiritual vigilance until leaving the body.

Swamiji was a master of being in the world, but not of it. With the tenderness of a mother's love for a newborn, he carefully instructed me how to live in that same way. In his inimical, serious, yet humorous way, he was able to use our adventure in Bombay as a vehicle to communicate the subtleties of playing in the awareness of the simultaneously nondual/dual world. Always giving and glowing, Swami Prakashananda Saraswati was a saint who greeted all with love and the joy of honoring the Divine in them.

One of the special qualities of this biography is that it is written by Harihar, the name given by Prakashananda to Titus Foster, who lived as his disciple at Sapta Shringh and in his humble two-room ashram in Nasik for eight years. Because of Harihar's long-term service to Prakashananda, he is able to communicate in this biography his first-hand knowledge and experience of his teachings and stories in a way that brings Prakashananda's shakti right through the pages. The delightful, personal narrative and the well-chosen use of Prakashananda's love and wisdom stories bring to us the essence of the Prakashananda experience. It is an experience and awareness worth knowing and treasuring.

Gabriel Cousens, M.D.
Author of *Sevenfold Peace, Conscious Eating,*
Spiritual Nutrition and The Rainbow Diet, and
Director of the Tree of Life Rejuvenation Center

Preface

The teachings of a spiritual master can be said to be influenced by two principal factors. First, by the "seed principles" which have flowered and matured within him and led him to spiritual illumination. Second, by the religious tradition in which he has evolved. Certainly, the symbolism a teacher uses and is familiar with will depend on his vehicle to spiritual realization, whether Buddhist, Muslim, Hindu, Christian, or Hebrew. However spiritually evolved he may be, a Saint or Jnani tends to remain faithful to his tradition and its symbolism, and more specifically, he tends to adhere strictly to the tradition of his particular lineage and culture.

When we look at Swamiji Prakashananda's teaching we see that his symbology is essentially Hindu and that he is a devotee of the Divine Mother. For Swamiji, life in the world with its good and bad, its joys and miseries, was the manifestation of the supreme principle called Shiva, which is the Absolute Reality beyond name and form, changeless and eternal and known as Sat (truth) Chit (consciousness) and Ananda (bliss).

Contained in the bosom of Absolute Reality (Shiva) is potential creation in the form of energy. This energy is one with Shiva like the two sides of the same coin. It is His creative power and it is called Shakti, Bhavagati, Jagadamba and many other such names. This energy is also known as the Divine Mother of the Universe who gives birth to all beings. The "Female" Principle, which emanates from the Shiva Principle, becomes the multifarious differentiated universe even as white light reflected in a prism becomes separated into different colors. The universe, therefore, is in essence, one with the absolute reality; and yet, in appearance, is other than Absolute Reality. The phenomenal world is often thought of by the Hindu mind as a cosmic illusion, "maya," or the Divine Leela or Game of the Absolute. The human being is born into this "illusion" and must find his or her way back to the undifferentiated light of the Absolute.

In practice, spiritual seekers or Sadhaks, are usually those who have, to some extent, awakened to the fact that the 'world,' with its suffering and confusion, is not their true home. They now start to struggle like a hooked fish. Partially awakened, they still have no means or understanding with which to extricate themselves from their predicament. They swim helplessly between the pairs of opposites: good and bad; light and darkness; unity and diversity, desperately looking for illumination. They are, at this point, acutely vulnerable to any false teacher or teaching that may try to snare them. They can only cry out in their heart for help. It is then that, if they are sincere, the universe will often respond by providing a meeting with a spiritual teacher or teaching. "When the disciple is ready, the guru appears" goes the saying.

"Gu" means darkness and "ru" means light. Guru means that principle that leads a seeker from darkness to light. Guru may come in any form but generally as an embodied human being no different from the disciple. Throughout the ages there have been such beings: Jesus, Buddha, Shankharacharya. They have all left behind teachings, either written by themselves or by their followers. These teachings are the result of direct revelation and by reading them and obeying their injunctions, the seeker can find suggestions as to how to return to his or her true home. One can also find oneself precipitated into a new kind of bondage; a maze of do's and dont's commonly known throughout history as a religion. What should be setting the seeker free can only too easily precipitate him or her into a different kind of bondage. The wake of persecution, violence and wars left in the aftermath of the world religions is known to us all. The thorn of teachings used to extricate the thorn of spiritual ignorance sometimes gets stuck in a person's flesh leaving him or her twice the discomfort and pain he or she had before. Therefore, there is an important emphasis placed on a self-realized teacher who can ensure that this does not happen.

Swami Prakashananda was not a self-appointed teacher. He never gave lectures or wrote any books. Nevertheless, because of his spiritual attainment, his words were imbued with the power and grace of the guru principle, the indwelling principle and presence which, being of God, guides a human being back to himself or herself. Prakashananda never pointed to himself but always to the guru principle within the seeker. He never looked for disciples, nor did he encourage any kind of organization to spring up around him. On the contrary, he encouraged seekers not to depend on structured organizations or even on the form of one particular teacher, but rather to recognize the guru within. This he did by his teaching in the form of direct instruction often in the form of parables, his example, and most of all, by the inspiration of his own being, by his love.

Swamiji delighted in being "agaram bagaram," an indefinable word meaning a mixture of hodgepodge-ness, rustic humor, simplicity and ironic self-deprecation. On many occasions, identifying himself with being agaram bagaram was deliberately used as a reason to remain apart from the politics and bustle of grand schemes, large organizations and power that, on occasions, were thrust in his direction.

This short biography is divided into two parts. Part I is a brief account of Swamiji's life. Part II is a compilation of his teachings and stories. Unless otherwise stated, the author's commentary appears in italics; all other text is Swamiji's words. The glossary translates unfamiliar words which are usually Sanskrit. These have been retained partly to preserve the original flavor of Babaji's words and partly because they often have no direct English translation. The first time a Sanskrit word appears, it will be italicized. 'Swamiji' and 'Babaji' both usually refer to Baba Prakashananda. The biographical details in Part I are mostly pieced together from Swamiji's reminiscences over a period of time and hopefully most of the main events of his life have been included.

The reader's indulgence is humbly requested for any glaring gaps, omissions, or errors. As in the famous story of the blind man describing the elephant in which the blind man perceives only a fraction of the totality, this biography claims to be no more than one blind man's perception of the mystery of the Absolute reflected in a great man (mahatma).

Finally, salutations to the guru principle, which is the inspiration for this book and which manifests through the saints. Salutations to Prakashananda!

Titus Foster (Harihar)

Introduction

Baba Prakashananda

I first met Baba Prakashananda walking along a garden path some fifty miles outside Bombay. He was dressed in the ochre-colored cotton robe of a monk and his presence, luminosity, and effortless, graceful simplicity shocked my hard cynical Western ego into silence. I knew myself to be in the presence of a Great Man.

I had heard that Baba Prakashananda was a Siddha—a perfected being—and somehow imagined he must be a sort of Superman who was powerful and self-sufficient and had transcended the pain, confusion, limitations and ups and downs of the mundane existence with which I was so familiar. During the ten years that followed, what was gradually revealed was something different. The self-sufficiency, transcendence, wisdom, and power were all there but Babaji was, in a sense, not the "owner" of these qualities. His interest lay elsewhere. In Love. It manifested visibly in his work with the children who lived in his ashram at Sapta Shringh and in the kindness, respect, and consideration he extended to all those he met, irrespective of their status in life.

Being around him in the close proximity of discipleship was never easy and Babaji was merciless in working on the selfishness which lay at the core of my pain. By the force of his spiritual realization he was able to kindle a kind of "holy fire" within me which was often excruciatingly painful as the darkness within was exposed again and again. The miracle that was born out of the ashes, however, was worth everything. What arose was a sense of God Itself, the Unknowable Essence and Source of Life. Gradually the Truth dawned. I had always somewhere known, but scarcely dared believe, that One Essence pervaded and animated everyone and everything. Under Babaji's protective eye, I started to partake in this new Understanding and his unconditional love allowed me to slowly let go of the protective walls of suspicion, fear, and mistrust I had erected against the world. At last I sensed and even shared in the Source of Babaji's outrageous love for the motley humanity which surrounded him. We were all One in God, in Love.

Titus Foster

Agaram Bagaram Baba

*Life, Teachings, and Parables—
A Spiritual Biography of
Baba Prakashananda*

PART I

LIFE

One hundred twenty miles northeast of the sweltering bustle of Bombay lies Nasik. It is a town of pilgrimage whose altitude of 2,000 feet makes it a relative haven from the oppressive humidity of Bombay.

The year is 1983. A man reclines bare-chested on a bed in a small upper room. He is in his late sixties and a full white beard adds a misleadingly comfortable benevolence to his face. The relaxed alertness of his demeanor has been won by hard years of asceticism and hardship; the lines of that hardship are hidden under the beard. To watch him sitting easily, greeting those who come to meet him, is to feel oneself in the court of a king, yet a king who knows no separation or difference from his court.

Inside his room sit a dozen visitors, men on one side, women on the other. His bed backs onto the wall and he greets visitors propped up on a cushion with legs outstretched. Although only in his late sixties, his years lie heavily on his body, now greatly reduced by his long years of asceticism and the illnesses that pursue him *relentlessly. Even now, his body has the potential of great strength and testifies to a previous practice of hatha yoga and other physical exercise. His muscular legs give witness to miles of arduous foot travel. His chest is powerful and his stomach pregnant with* kumbak *and spiritual power. He wears thick-lensed glasses which shield luminous eyes animated with an indefinable certainty.*

Immediately next to his chair is a table on which sits a bronze statue of the 18-armed Divine Mother; next to Her sit Hanuman *and* Dattatreya. *Underneath, a brass cobra rises from a* Shiva Lingam. *The central position of his* puja *is occupied by a large statue of his* guru. *Close at hand are two favorite companions:* Kum Kum, *which he applies to the foreheads of visitors with the blessing "AMBA Mata Ki Jai!" (victory to the Divine Mother) and a steel tin of chewing tobacco; a wad is almost always in his mouth, pushed up on one side of his cheek.*

He is totally at ease with himself and others, his expression a fluid, moving kaleidoscope of joy, love, laughter, mischief, or anger, depending on his mood. In this court, the only law is love, which vibrates tangibly in the room. He bears the ochre cloth of a monk (Swami) and the name 'Prakashananda,' meaning the joy of the light of awareness. Visitors, however, address him as Babaji, meaning father, or as Swamiji.

Every day he meets people, holding court with many, each of whom comes for a different reason. One person comes to ask for a blessing or remedy for ill health, another to increase his wealth, others to ask for a child or perhaps for spiritual instruction. Some come only because they love Swamiji. They simply sit and watch the courtroom drama unfold scene by scene. Outside are the sounds of rickshaws, cycle bells, and the shouts of children playing. The Muslim call to prayer is heard close by. There is a mosque a hundred yards away and a Christian church next door. In contrast to the clamor outside, there is an almost womb-like stillness in the room that envelops visitors like a warm, benevolent cocoon. An almost tangible lightness and sweetness permeate the air. A fan swishes the hot air around the room.

Suddenly a lady and young girl who is her sister-in-law enter the room and sit straight in front of Swamiji's chair in urgent supplication. They have obviously come for something. Almost immediately two things happen before a word is exchanged. The door behind them opens and an old-time disciple enters the room with a tiffin carrier in hand containing cooked food for Swamiji. In the same instant the telephone rings summoning Swamiji into the next room. It is the head of a major government department in Bombay informing Swamiji how happy he is that his son's marriage date is definite.

Swamiji re-enters the room having answered the call. He looks inquiringly at the two women. The elder speaks.

"Swamiji, my sister-in-law here has not been able to find a marriage suit despite every effort," she laments.

Swamiji's reply is instantaneous.

"God will give! There is no doubt about it. This tiffin carrier and the phone call are your answer."

His attitude is one of total certainty that as God's universe is perfect, the unusual sequence of these events within life itself have replied to the question.

The women's faces at first register hesitation and then finally total delight. Moreover, a dawning understanding that somehow the phone call represents affirmation to the question and the tiffin carrier represents the blessing of plenty. They too have been inadvertently drawn for a moment into viewing the world from a totally different perspective—the perspective of a jnani, for whom the universe unfolds itself with perfect simplicity second by second, revealing its secrets to those with the eyes to see. The women get up to leave and in parting, the older woman, thinking that fortune is smiling, turns back, hoping for another miracle.

"Swamiji, my legs are paining and I can't walk properly!"

Swamiji replies with humor and compassion.

"Neither can I, mother! What to do?"

The perspective of a jnani, for whom the Universe unfolds with perfect simplicity second by second, revealing its secrets to those with eyes to see.

The Jnani: *Who is Prakashananda?*

*"The jnani is like the fragrant flower
which doesn't need to advertise its
nectar: the bees come automatically."*

*Who is Prakashananda? Who is a jnani? To describe the life
and mind of a great soul, a jnani, is to catch a glimpse of the ultimate
potential and mystery of every one of us. The jnani is one who has
entered into the essence behind all religions and encompasses and
embodies them all. By perceiving that the self-existent and immortal
supreme principle pointed to in all religions exists within the jnani
himself or herself, and, indeed, constitutes his innermost being, the
jnani transcends all relative philosophies, dogmas, ideas and even
religious forms. He becomes universal and a conductor or channel for
that very supreme principle (*guru tattva*). He becomes a master, a
Sadguru, a transparency for the mystery of God. Prakashananda
says:*

Some are born jnanis and the reason is that they have done *tapasya*
in past existences. They are born for a reason: to give happiness to
the world and to show a path to mankind. A jnani is one whose soul
light (*atmajyoti*) is blazing; when we come into contact with him or

her, the quintessential spiritual knowledge, that rarefied *jnan*, kindles our own dormant inner knowledge. Hence the hymn 'Jyota se jyota jagavo, sadguru jyota se jyota jagavo; mera antara timira mitavo, sadguru jyota se jyotaa jagavo.' (Oh, *sadguru*, light my soul's light with your light.)

Understand that when we revere a saint or jnani, it is the spiritual knowledge that manifests through his body that we revere, not his body or personality. Look at Baba (Muktananda); that jnan existed before he took birth and it will be there eternally. While he was alive his body was a channel for that jnan and it is this we revere, not his body. That is why we place his books on the *puja* because they contain Baba's jnan in written form *(a reference to Prakashananda's occasional habit of keeping scriptural texts as puja items.)* Look at a match. Although it contains potential fire, its only on contact with a matchbox that fire actually manifests. Similarly, in all of us the supreme knowledge is sleeping, and on contact with a Sadguru, it awakens. Don't forget, it is the flame that is important, not the match stick. Likewise, it is the soul light (atmajyoti) within a man that is important, which uses the body and manifests through it. When the body is burned out the *atma* discards the body and finds a new vehicle for its manifestation.

In this world good and bad exist side by side; black smoke exists together with the bright flame; however, we should contemplate the flame, not the smoke. A lake's bottom is mud, but put a tiny lotus seed in that mud and a lotus emerges from it so beautiful that *Laxmi* Herself stands on it. Now, if I tell people the truth, who will listen? If I tell you that this here *(the material world)* is hell, who would believe it? But it is true. However, from this dirt also grows a lotus. In our body, dirt is below and beauty is above. The *kundalini shakti* has her root or seat down amid the dirt; she sits between the anus and the sex organ, but flowers up above in the head. All the great jnanis are like that; they are born from the sexual fluids of man and woman, but their consciousness flowers above, in freedom. That's why the jnani is like the fragrant flower which doesn't need to advertise its nectar; the bees come automatically.

6

King Janaka and Ashtavakra

A jnani, or knower of the Self, comes in many guises and is often unrecognized by the world. An example is Ashtavakra in the following stories.

King Janaka was a great and powerful king but one night he had a vivid dream which greatly disturbed him. He found himself as a beggar having had no food for 15 days. At last he came to a *dharamsala* (a shelter for pilgrims) but it was closing as he arrived. Literally dying and with his last remaining strength, he begged that the bowl from which alms had been distributed be scraped and given to him. Grudgingly this was done and he found himself with a little *khichari* in his tin plate. He staggered weakly to the nearby field and sat down to eat. However, in that field two bulls were fighting and on seeing him, one of the bulls charged at him and tossed the food up into the air, scattering it. In horror, his eyes jerked open to find that he was King Janaka and that he was, in fact, lying in a royal bed being fanned by his Queens. Closing his eyes, again he was the dying beggar confronted by the bull. With a moan he again opened his eyes and became the King.

Janaka now became a man obsessed. Out of the two identities was one really more real than the other? He issued a proclamation to his kingdom that all the great sages of the land should come to his court in order to interpret his dream. Not one could do so and furious, he had them all imprisoned.

Now one of the sages had a son who was deformed in eight places, hence his name Ashtavakra (eight distortions). On learning that his father was in prison, he set out for King Janaka's court. This court was a magnificent affair. Upon seeing the lad boldly enter the grand court with the peculiar jerking movement caused by his deformity, the entire court, including the King, burst out laughing. To the astonishment of the assembly, Ashtavakra himself then laughed loudly, whereupon a sudden hush came over the court.

7

"Who are you, lad, and what are you laughing at?" asked Janaka.

"I had heard such great things about the splendor and wisdom of King Janaka and his court but I now see you are just a pack of leather merchants. When you see me you only see the external skin and deformity of my body and are blind to the spirit which animates it. Now, ask your question so that my father can go free," said Ashtavakra.

Astonished at the boy's authority and spiritual radiance, the King explained his dream.

Ashtavakra replied, "King, when you are a beggar in your dream being a king isn't a reality for you and when you are a king being a beggar is also not a reality. In fact, neither identity is real. Reality is that from which both identities are projected—the pure, absolute witness, the Self."

The force of the words of a jnani was such that Janaka's confusion vanished. His mind was enlightened.

It is said that in the jnani, God and man, and heaven and earth, meet. In the life and teaching of such a being, we catch glimpses of the truth of which we are all part. If this account of Prakashananda's life and teachings gives the reader a glimpse of this truth, then surely its purpose is fulfilled. Therefore, let us allow Prakashananda, the bliss of the supreme light, to reveal himself—as the Divine presence within our own hearts.

2

Prakashananda's Early Life

"First God, then food."

In November 1917 Swamiji was born into a Brahmin family
in Karnataka, South India, and given the name Laxmi Narayan.
He said little about his early life. A sannyasi, it is said, has no past
and seldom mentions it. An exception to this was one of his earliest
memories as a child age eight when there occurred a preview of what
was to come in later years. He had been lying in bed half asleep and
had seen a vision of a large red face with many arms which awoke
a strange feeling in his heart. The vision stayed for a minute or two
and disappeared. This was, he said, his first darshan of the
eighteened-armed Goddess of Sapta Shringh he was destined to
meet years later and recognize as his true mother.

Early pictures of him show a handsome, finely proportioned
young man with intense burning eyes and a fair complexion not
usually associated with South India. We know that as a very young
man he left home in Karnataka, South India, with a profound faith
in Mahatma Gandhi and the Independence Movement, which he
joined. Indeed, for a while he even enjoyed British hospitality in a

political jail! Sometimes he remembered with a certain admiration the good food he and the other prisoners were served and how well they were treated.

However, after Independence in 1948, Laxmi Narayan gradually became disgusted with politics as he realized that, after all, a number of those who had taken part in the Independence Movement and had striven to dislodge British rule were only too human in their weaknesses and desire for the trappings, pomp, and power of those of whom they wished to be rid.

Disillusioned, he started wandering around India looking for that which lies beyond human limitation and weakness: God, the supreme fulfillment. Three times he completed entire circuits around India, one of them on foot, going as far north as Mount Kailas and Lake Manasaror in Tibet and south to Kanya Kumari. In his travels he met many different kinds of people and learned something from each of them. Sometimes he had money, often earned from his knowledge of astrology, and sometimes he had none, having to rely entirely on providence and the will of God. Often he went hungry, as his principle was never to ask for anything. This experience affected him profoundly and left him with a great love of feeding people, which culminated years later in founding an ashram dedicated to housing and feeding poor children.

One day in 1983 Kirin Narayan was researching her book based on Babaji's stories, Storytellers, Saints, and Scoundrels, *and recorded Swamiji reminiscing about those early years. In the recording, we follow the young Laxmi Narayan passing through various life experiences and witness his gradual transformation. We see his idealistic allegiance to the Congress Party and willingness to die for the truth he believed in give way to a profound devotion to ultimate truth rather than secular ideology. In these reminiscences we catch a unique, fascinating, delightful insight into the mind, humor, heart, and world of the intense, guileless young man who was later to become Swami Prakashananda.*

Babaji as a young man.

I was about eighteen when I left home. Why did I leave? My mother died when I was about ten, and one day I left home. At that time I was infatuated with the ideals of the Congress Party and thought of Gandhiji as a God, although I did not at that time revere God at all. Finally, I decided to set out to find out and explore for myself whether God was real or not and every day I used to spread my *asan* and meditate. I must have been in my early twenties at that time.

A relative of Swami Chidananda of the Shivananda ashram in Rishikesh met me and gave me a *mantra*. He advised me that if I were really interested in finding God, that I could go to one of three places where there were living masters who could guide me correctly. One was Hamsadev in Gujerat, one was Shivananda in Rishikesh and one was Nityananda in Vrajreshwari. These three gurus he told me about, but being independent I did not go to any of them. I took a train to Poona. From Poona I tried to get a ticket to Kashi (Banaras). At Kalyan I found I did not have enough money for a ticket all the way to Banaras, so I pawned my watch for about ten rupees and bought the ticket. So there I was on my way to Kashi!

I was warned before I arrived in Kashi that the priests there will rob you for four *annas*; their reputation was that bad. I found a place to sleep but food became a problem as I was a strict *Brahmin*. Also, I knew very little Hindi, only what I had learned during my association with the Congress Party. This must have been about 1939 or 1940. Everything was very cheap in India in those days but I could not eat just anywhere because I would not eat without being certain of the purity of the food, so I went hungry.

I met a Brahmin who said he would take me everywhere for one anna. That seemed reasonable enough so I entered into contract with him. We started out to see Banaras. He took me around saying 'Worship here for your mother, honor this image,' and so on until fairly soon I had virtually no money. I was stranded and penniless. A *sadhu* came up and offered to help me. He was wearing saffron (the color worn by a renunciant). I distrusted all Sadhus because, being a staunch member of the Congress, I was convinced that all those who wear saffron were thieves or cheats. But he persisted in calling me and when I told him to go, he wouldn't leave me. After I had been arguing with him for over a half hour, a *Brahmachari* came up wearing a white cloth. I preferred the look of him in his clean white clothing.

'What is your guru's name?' I asked.

'Satyanarayana Maharaj,' he answered. His own name was Shankar Ananda Bharati. He said, 'Come along and I will take you to my guru.'

He took me there and his guru asked who I was and where I had come from. 'I am here to become your disciple,' I answered. 'Tell me what a disciple does. How do I become a disciple?'

He answered, 'There are three ways. We can arrange for you to study English, and to study Sanscrit, or to become a *sanyassi*. You can choose whichever direction appeals to you. You decide which path you want and then you take it.'

This won't do for me, I thought. 'Just give me a mantra,' I told him. 'I am not going to shave my head, and I am not going to wear saffron. Just give me a place to stay, not even food or water. Give me a place and I will sit there without food or water until I see God. Can you give me a mantra by which I can accomplish that? I have come all the way to Kashi to see God. If I do your work will I see God? If I am just going to work I might as well work for wages elsewhere.'

'No,' he said, 'it cannot be like that. Without shaving your head and without doing our work, we cannot keep you here.'

Then I asked him, 'Have you seen God yourself?'

'No,' he answered truthfully.

'So,' I said, 'if you have not seen God yourself, how are you going to show me?'

I left. I still had about a rupee, which saw me to Allahabad. I traveled with a Madrasi whom I had met. We stayed in a *dharamsala* and in the morning after we had tea we decided to sell our gold earrings. People kept looking at them, either out of curiosity or because they were planning to steal them, we couldn't tell which, so we thought we should rid ourselves of those dangerous controversial objects. Then we went straight to the Nehru residence. I thought if I was not going to find God, I might as well stay with the Congress Movement. But that day Chiang Kai Shek had come to India and Nehru had gone to Delhi to meet him.

I met a lot of the great Congress leaders who were staying there, Nariman, Munshi, I saw them all. I said I would like to stay there.

I was skilled at spinning and wore only cloth woven from the cotton I had spun for myself. I demonstrated how well I could spin and told them about weaving centers I had organized in the South. I could take out a ninety count thread, which is very fine.

'Stay,' they said, as they were pleased, 'and meet Nehru when he returns tonight.'

But after an hour I felt like leaving, so I went to the station.

Hard Times

Then followed a period of wandering in which the young Laxmi Narayan passed through many life experiences. Hunger, destitution, and even arrest by the British were just a few of the experiences and they served to temper his character like iron in a furnace. He met saints and sinners and learned something from them all.

Finally, in Darwar, I took a job in a shop. When I have enough money, I thought, I will go on. I went into the shop and told the man I would work for my food and eight annas a day until I had enough money to go on. I had no idea where I would go. He agreed, so I worked for eighteen days until I had the money for a ticket to Bangalore. In Bangalore I did the same thing, working until I had money to go to Sailam. In Sailam I ran out of money and could not find work, so I left there on foot eating the leaves from tamarind trees with only water to drink.

Sometimes someone gave me something, sometimes not. I was disappointed in the ideals of the Congress and I had not found God. I used to stay five or six days in one place and then move on.

Near Dindugal there is a temple of the Goddess at Maddiguddi up on a high rock where I slept. At night ghosts and spirits hold dominion there and they manifested all around me, but I was completely unafraid.

In the morning I started off to Madurai. The road that leads from Dindugal to Madurai is very beautiful, and huge old tamarind trees shade the road on either side. About five miles outside Madurai I stopped to drink water at a small tank. Approaching the well I tucked my *lungi* and held out my hand to catch the water that was pouring out. As I tucked up the lungi, the fabric split from behind. My lungi tore so I could not wear it properly and I had no other, only a long shirt. My lungi had split exactly in half. I tied one half around my waist but it was not long enough to show beneath my shirt. To avoid looking naked, I removed my shirt, bundled it up under my arm, and threw the other half of the lungi over my shoulder. My only other possession was an old cigarette tin which I used for water. Carrying only that and dressed in this manner, I entered the great city of Madurai.

Meeting with a Jnani in Madurai

Madurai is a large city centered around the extensive ancient temple of the Goddess Meenakshi. Just the space enclosed in the *Nandi Mandap* of that temple can sleep over four thousand people. Near the temple the government has provided bathrooms for the public that are as well and beautifully built as temples. I went into one and bathed and washed those bits of cloth of mine.

I walked back to the center of the town, to the temple, and sat in the square around the sacred compound near the temple of Meenakshi. There is a custom there that before opening their shops in the morning many of the shopkeepers give charity in the form of

15

chits, coupons that can be exchanged for a meal or snack. I was sitting there watching fifty or sixty sadhus about a hundred feet away from me scramble for the six meal tickets that one merchant was distributing. I sat at a distance watching the play, seeing those sadhus in saffron push and grab and shout, laughing to myself with my hand under my chin and thinking, 'look what the world does for food.'

An old sadhu, a *mahatma*, came up beside me and said, 'I'll get you a coupon.'

'For what?' I asked.

'For food,' he said.

'I have no need of that.'

'Why?' he asked, 'Don't you eat?'

'Of course I eat, how could I have gotten so big without food?' I answered arrogantly. 'But I don't need food now. I am not eating.'

'Why?' he asked.

'First I want to see God, then I'll eat.' He asked me where I had been and I answered 'Kashi bashi, I have been all around.'

'Hasn't anyone been able to show you God?' he asked.

'No,' I said.

'Why? There are good mahatmas in Kashi.'

'No,' I answered. 'They were all sinners. Everyone was out to rob me.'

I told him a few of the incidents from my experience. After a time, he said, 'Well, what no one has shown you, I will show you. I will show you so that you will be able to eat again. Now first let us eat.'

'No.' I was adamant. 'First God and then food.'

Actually I had been practicing meditation all this time and had seen a star, a brilliant point of light. Patiently, the old mahatma began to question me.

'Is the seed in the tree or the tree in the seed?'

I was silent.

'Answer me. Is the seed in the tree or not?'

I could find no answer so he went on to explain.

'In all trees there are seeds. Without seed no tree comes into being. Where is the seed? It is potential within each tree. If the tree is not watered it will die. How long will a sapling live without water? In a few days it will die and when it is dead there is neither tree nor seed. If one wants the fruit, the seed, one must protect and nourish the tree. At the proper time, in the appointed season, the tree will bear fruit, but never without having been protected and cared for. In this same manner, God is potential within you. If you want to realize Him, you must protect and nourish your body and you will have to continuously repeat the mantra you receive from a guru. Then from within, God will become pleased and His pleasure will manifest in you.'

In this manner he gave me understanding and then there in Madurai, in the temple of Meenakshi, he gave the mantra to me. For three months we traveled together from there, visiting all the holy places in the southern tip of India, such as Rameshwaram, Kanya Kumari, and so on.

Once in Rameshwaram we were sitting outside a house under a tree. The people were known to us there and in the most friendly and hospitable manner had prepared food for us. We had all eaten and the banana leaves from which we had all eaten had been thrown out onto the rubbish heap. Although no food was left on the leaves, four dogs fought over the rubbish for their share. Then a beggar came up, and beating off the dogs, picked up a leaf and began to lick it.

'See,' said my Babaji, 'truth and falsehood, rules and cleanliness. The soul makes no distinction when the body is hungry. In times of hunger all discrimination falls away. Understanding this, in the future you should give food. It is with this understanding that you should feed others. Understand that all souls are your own. All living beings experience hunger and require nourishment. At some time in the future you should provide this. God sits in the heart of all beings. Whoever you feed, that offering reaches God. Give to the hungry and the poor without distinction of caste or custom.'[1]

[1]Author's note: We can judge the impression this teaching had on the young Laxmi-Narayan in view of his later commitment to feeding others on a large scale at Sapta Shringh.

In this manner for three months he used each sight to teach me as we walked on pilgrimage. In some places people called us and honored us, fed us and gave us gifts, and in other places not, but everywhere we moved in joy. After three months we reached Palni and there he instructed me.

'Now you must find work. You must not waste your life begging. Continue to remember God and you will find Him.'

At first I was not able to find employment because I was not well-dressed or shaved, so he gave me money for a shave and a new *dhoti* and then I was able to find a job in a shop. What wages? Three rupees. What work? Carrying water. It was all right. Following the guru's orders, I continued to serve. However, after two or three months, I became ill with blood dysentery. I had to go forty or fifty times a day. My employer gave me some medicines but they were not effective. He was unwilling to spare me from work but after some time I was physically unable to work. I was too weak even to reach the bathroom and so he took pity on me and gave me a place to rest. I became seriously ill so they took me to a hospital thinking I was about to die. The doctor there turned out to be a caste fellow of mine. He gave me excellent medical treatment, kept me in a special ward and paid attention to my case. He noted my name and found out where my home was and after contacting my family and receiving some news from my home, he took even better care of me. After eighteen days, when I was well enough to leave, they came and took me back home.

Satyagraha and Prison

After some days at home, I left for Mysore where the Congress movement was active. I got back into the Independence movement and was friends with many of the leaders. Every day orders were given for *satyagraha* and every day there were reports of activity, but it was untrue. No one ever really went because they were being beaten on the way and they were all scared.

'Good,' I said, 'I will go. You can only die once, not over and over.'

So at a mass meeting, in front of a crowd of four thousand people, I volunteered and others joined me. Nine of us gave our names and in front of all those people our names were announced. The leaders all came and argued with me.

'We cannot allow you to go. This is Mysore and we should go first or they will honor you and respect you more than us. Do you have funds for your expenses?'

'I have no need of money,' I replied. 'We will take alms as we go and accomplish our satyagraha like that with the support of the people on the way. I don't require your permission and I don't require your funds and I don't need your support. I am going right ahead with my plans.'

Hearing this, the Congress president of that area came and joined our party. Due to his leadership there were thirty-two of us when we set out.

Our group moved on to the next *zilla* where four or five people who were important and well-known in that place courted arrest. At night, if you gave a speech, you were arrested. The rest of us would move ahead toward Mysore. Each day another batch of *satyagris* would move through the area. I took one man and went ahead to prepare for our party. All but the two of us were arrested. We waited and then caught a ride back and questioned the police, who informed us that we would also be arrested. They took us themselves to the place where we were to be arrested. There was a big riot going on there and the whole town of forty or fifty thousand was out. Later, as we were being taken away, my father and brother came and tried to take me home. I refused, saying that I would not return home until my country was free.

The police officers in that area were all friends of my family's. They refused to arrest me.

'Do what you like,' they said, 'we will not arrest you. No one in this district will arrest you unless you do something really illegal like cutting down a sandalwood tree.'

The next day nine of us collected nine axes and took out a procession to advertise our intention of cutting down some government sandalwood trees. We didn't actually cut down any trees, we just said we were going to, but still no one came forward to arrest us. When our procession had gotten half a mile beyond the town we flagged down a car. We got a ride to another town about thirty miles ahead where three people had been shot and there was a curfew in force. Strict rules had been passed and the police had been ordered not even to give water to the Congress prisoners.

While we were in that town we just took off our Congress hats. Only by our hats could we be identified as Congress members. We made full inquiries, as this was another district, and found out that they were taking people two miles outside town and beating them up.

Two of the other men with me heard this and fled, saying, 'We don't want to come along. We don't want to be beaten!'

The next day we let it be known that we planned to leave for Mysore at four o'clock by a particular route. At three we started out by another route. We said four but we left at three. Just outside the town we stopped a car and rode in it. The police were stopping cars and looking for us. At Shri Rangapatam there was a curfew and the motor bridge over the Kaveri River was blocked by police at both ends. All the vehicles from all over Mysore were being checked thoroughly and all suspicious characters were being beaten up on the spot. Because of this, we stopped at a village at about eleven at night. A man came and directed us to a place where we would be fed by the Congress volunteers of that area. It rained heavily all that day. We sat there and thought about finding a way across the river. About three hundred people trying to cross in boats had been intercepted. What was to be done?

'How will you go?' we were asked. 'The police are beating everybody up. You had better turn back.'

But Mysore was only fourteen miles away.

'If I die,' I said, 'I die. When you get born, you are bound to die sometime. I am going to Mysore.'

When we got about half a mile down the road, a police car drew up next to us. The inspector in that car was called Mustafa. I still remember his name.

'Where are you people going?' he asked.

'Mysore,' I said.

'Arrest them all,' he commanded.

So they arrested us all. One of our party was the son of an influential millionaire. They asked him where he was going and he said, 'To my wedding.'

They could see by his dress that he was lying and beat him over the head with a stick. The blow broke his skin and he began to bleed.

'You demons! You have made me bleed!' The rich man's son was indignant.

Hearing this the police began to laugh and with the laughter their anger was spent. They took us off to Shri Rangapatam and detained us. The first day they tried to reason with us. We refused to listen and remained in the jail. So they detained us. We organized ourselves and appointed a spokesman for the detainees. We were not properly fed so we organized a one-day fast for better food. As a result, some of us were transferred to the jail in Bangalore where two thousand people were already being held, of whom nine hundred were detainees. Soon a separate camp was set up at Whitefields where we were all cared for as first class prisoners. We were still there when Independence was achieved and we were released. Many of my fellow prisoners later became important politicians in the Congress party and I could have done the same.

Further Wandering

All this time I was still searching for God. My wanderings took me to Goa where I spent several years. There I was not involved in politics but in religion. I became known as a soothsayer and an astrologer by telling a truth to someone who would then bring his friends. I earned a lot and so every few months I would set out on pilgrimage from there. I earned so much that after a year I began to give predictions free. In that manner I spent over two years there and during that time, buying my tickets, I traveled all over India from the Himalayas to Kanya Kumari, the southern tip of India.

I will relate just one incident—so many things happened during those years and on my travels—to illustrate my powers at that time. There was a girl of about sixteen who was dying. The doctors could do nothing for her. Her mouth could not be forced open and she was near death. Her family came to seek my advice. I saw that something from outside was affecting her.

'I will do what I can,' I told them, 'bring me a lemon. I will know with one lemon if she can survive.'

I took that lemon and prayed. I prayed to all the deities and saints of whom I had ever heard. Nityananda's name was a part of my prayers even at that time. I did all this just as it come into my head spontaneously.

I cut the lemon and showed them how to force it into her mouth and kept the other half for the next day. But by the next day she had come round and asked for tea. No other medicines, just a lemon and the name of God. I am describing just one miracle but my reputation was based on many. They called me a man of God!

> From Goa, Laxmi Narayan went to spend some time at Gangapur, a spot sacred to Dattatreya and it was here that he first heard about a mountain sacred to the Divine Mother. Its name was Sapta Shringh and an extraordinary destiny awaited him there which was to influence the lives of many people as well as completely transform him. One day in 1953 he came to the little-known mountain of Sapta Shringh about 40 miles north of Nasik in Maharashtra and his wandering ceased forever.

**The mountain of Sapta Shringh
and the temple of the Mother.**

3

Sapta Shringh 1953–1980

"Sapta Shringh is a physical
representation of the Divine Power."

Sapta Shringh is part of a long line of mountains stretching north
into Gujerat and south joining the Western Ghats. The mountain
of Sapta Shringh itself stands over 4,000 feet, a 'Shakti Peeth'
sacred to the Divine Mother for thousands of years. Its origins as a
Shakti Peeth go back to the ancient sage Markendeya, who
performing tapas on the adjoining mountain, realized the primordial rock of Sapta Shringh which majestically faced him, to be the
Diving Power made manifest. This vertical sliver of rock which rises
from the 4,000-foot plateau is nearly two miles long and seems to
be tilted slightly as if listening to Markendeya's hymns of praise and
longing. The temple of the mother is plugged into the rock like a light
bulb in order to manifest light to the devotees.

It was also where Matsyendranath, the founder of the famous
'Nath' tradition, did penance. The Naths produced such exalted
saints as Jnaneshwar Maharaj, who is one of the most important
figures in the Marathi mystical tradition. It is significant that the
Naths are exponents of the science of Siddha Yoga, one of whose

adepts was Swami Muktananda Paramahamsa, who was later to become Laxmi Narayan's guru.

So it was that in about 1953 destiny finally brought Laxmi Narayan to the long, winding, three-and-one-half-mile path leading from the plain to this same mountain of Sapta Shringh and up to the 4,000-foot plateau, or 'gadh,' with its stupendous view of the plains stretched out below. Mounting the last 200-odd steps leading up to the temple, he finally stood in front of the Divine Mother. As he gazed at the red, eighteen-armed figure a flower decorating Her detached itself and fell, striking him. A profound experience occurred in which he recognized the image he had seen so many years before as a child.

After all those years of seeking, Laxmi Narayan had come home. He was to remain in Sapta Shringh for 27 years. In the past a huge boulder had detached itself from the towering rock and crashed down to the plateau. It was from this rock that a cave had been fashioned, and here Laxmi Narayan now lived and meditated on the Mother whose form loomed above him. This cave, called Nagendra cave, stands a few yards from the perimeter of what later became his ashram.

The process of transformation from the human earthly consciousness to divine consciousness now began in earnest. About his actual sadhana *with its hardships, joys, disappointments and eventual realization we can only guess, but the utter simplicity of the first three years he spent in Nagendra cave can be inferred from his own brief description.*

My habit whilst in that cave was to go to the Ganga Jamuna pool which was one-half mile distant to take my bath and bring two buckets of water back to the cave. Any excess was used on the tomatoes I had planted. A tiger used to come and sit on one of the rocks near the cave. In those days tigers roamed freely.

"A picture flashed in my mind—the red face I had seen as a child. I broke down and wept."

His food often consisted of fruit and leaves. It was for Laxmi Narayan the time of his great penance. Having found his true Mother in the Divine Mother Herself, he surrendered himself to Her, mind, body, and soul, as Markendeya had done before him on the neighboring mountain thousands of years ago. From his very occasional remarks about those days, we know he often addressed his burning devotion to the Divine Mother in the form of the "Kunjika Stotra." This hymn of praise to the Divine Mother is revealed by Shiva to Parvati, in which he explains that for one who has no knowledge or means of puja or ritual at his disposal, it is enough merely to recite the Siddha Kunjika hymn, which is itself complete as the key of liberation. Once Swamiji mentioned how one day the sound of the omnipresent cosmic vibration—nada— revealed itself to him and indeed, never left his awareness.

Perhaps his realization and experience at that time expresses itself best in his own comments on the true significance of Sapta Shringh, about which he would say the following.

Christians go to church, Muslims go to the mosque, so we should also visit the Divine Mother at least once a month, on the full moon day.[2] One life force works through the body, speaking through the mouth, smelling through the nose, hearing through the ears, seizing through the hands, and excreting through the anus. Similarly, in the world, different places represent different manifestations of the one divine power or spirit. Sapta Shringh is the abode of Raja Rajeshwari, meaning king of kings. The yogis know Her to dwell within and call Her *Kundalini*. The *Nath Panthis* gave the mountain the name Sapta Shringh, symbolizing the seven chakras (energy centers) through which Kundalini passes. The seventh chakra is called *sahasrar*, the thousand-petaled lotus, and when she reaches there, a nectar falls. This is symbolized by the half moon on the statue, and the snake at the top of her head is Kundalini. When the individual soul drinks that nectar, it becomes immortal, returns to universal consciousness and

---

[2] The purnima, or full moon day, is sacred to the Mother.

never again suffers in the cycle of birth and death. Shiva, the supreme consciousness or plenitude, dwells in the sahasrar, and when the individual soul re-unites with Him, it attains *moksha* or liberation.

The mountain of Sapta Shringh is a physical manifestation of the divine power, the Shakti. If you look at a *Shri Yantra*, you will see that the *bindu* (point) in the middle and the various geometrical points are represented physically by Sapta Shringh as the central bindu, and by the various mountains in a fifteen-mile radius, which represent the geometrical points of the yantra.

4

Gurudiksha 1956

Initiation

In 1956 a momentous meeting took place for Laxmi Narayan. On one of his occasional visits to Yeola, a town about 50 miles east of Nasik, Laxmi Narayan was told of a "true sadhu" also from Karnataka, his own birthplace. He lived very simply three miles away in a tiny hamlet called Suki. As it happened, the "true sadhu" turned out to be none other than Swami Muktananda Paramahamsa (Baba). He was a disciple of the great Swami Nityananda of Ganeshpuri. Baba was later to settle in Ganeshpuri himself, founding an ashram called Gurudev Siddha Peeth in memory of Nityananda, which was to attract thousands of seekers from all over the world. Swamiji later described the meeting quite casually.

On arrival in Suki I saw Baba reclining on a swing with a few devotees sitting close by. I paid my respects and sat down. Suddenly the devotees came and started touching my feet.

I told them, 'Touch your guru's feet, not mine.'
They replied, 'Our guru has told us to touch yours.'

Indeed, the mutual love and respect born at that first meeting must have been very great because the same evening, after the devotees had departed leaving the two together, Laxmi Narayan requested Baba to initiate him as his guru. It is interesting to note that not only did Baba initiate him that very night, but also returned Laxmi Narayan's humble dakshina with a handful of coins offered to the padukas of his own guru Nityananda. Laxmi Narayan, however, insisted that his guru should accept the dakshina, however modest.

Baba instructed, 'Come to Ganeshpuri when I call you, meanwhile return to Sapta Shringh. It's a good place.'

The 'good place' was at that time a tiny collection of buildings housing a few brahmins and a small number of very poor tribal people.

I heard nothing from Baba for a while. Then, quite some time later in Sapta Shringh, some pilgrims visited and I offered them what hospitality I could. They told me their guru had sent them on a pilgrimage, so I asked him his name.

'Swami Muktananda of Ganeshpuri,' was the reply.

I told them he was also mine! They reported back to Baba and soon afterward he called me to Ganeshpuri. It was the first of many visits.

Great closeness was destined to develop between them. It was quite soon after this encounter that a second meeting took place with Swami Janananda, another famous disciple of Swami Nityananda, about whom Babaji was later to say, "He who has seen Swami Janananda has seen Nityananda."

About that time I was thinking of building a small hut to live in at Sapta Shringh, but the funds weren't available. One day a certain man took me to Nasik for the darshan of Swami Janananda, Bhagawan Nityananda's disciple who runs the Nityananda Ashram in Kanangaard, Karnataka. In the evening we went to meet him and he spoke lovingly to me. I asked him about the route to *Kailas* and *Manasaror*, which he himself had visited. He told me the route he'd taken and the difficulties he'd encountered. He then invited me to take food and in the evening there was a film on Nityananda. The following day I took leave of Swamiji and returned to Sapta Shringh. It so happened that the man who had accompanied me gave me 100 rupees and that was enough to start work on my hut!

Founding the Ashram

After completion, however, the hut was found to leak so badly in the monsoon that Laxmi Narayan slept and meditated on raised boxes. The three-and-one-half-month monsoon in Sapta Shringh is notorious and the 4,500-foot mountain often stays under clouds for days at a time, leaving an almost permanent film of damp on everything.

Gradually Laxmi Narayan's spiritual destiny started to unfold and manifest itself, attracting an ever-expanding nucleus of devotees. An ashram was soon to emerge out of that solitary, leaking room.

It was my habit from the earliest days to distribute prasad to the adivasi children, and seeing it, people started offering the facilities for their proper feeding. A dharamsala sprang up and finally a small ashram, which included a children's hostel and a small school. The ashram we called Sapta Shringh Gurudev Ashram. Sapta Shringh in honor of the Mother and Gurudev in honor of all the great mahatmas who have done penance there. Originally we thought of providing the children with three meals a day. However, this idea was put aside as it encouraged the villagers to be idle, as they didn't then have to work to feed their own children! So we gave them only breakfast and lunch.

33

Soon poor children from the neighboring villages came and stayed with us. They were given free board and lodging and education at the school. The government offered us financial help, but I refused, saying, 'The government has only two hands, whereas the Mother has a thousand!'

The ashram has continued up to the present day and now houses about fifty poor children. A visitor can witness the moving sight of anywhere up to one hundred twenty-five children being served breakfast and lunch, as well as a small evening prasad, in the ashram hall every day of the year.

"Bal Bhojan" was officially inaugurated by Swami Muktananda in 1960 and the events that accompanied the opening inaugurations and yagna were a sign of what lay in the future.

In the middle of the *Nauchandi Yagna* a man arrived with a silver statue of the Sapta Shringh Devi, which he presented to me. He explained that he had ordered the statue to be made in Nasik for himself, but that in a dream, the Mother had told him to give it to the sadhu at Sapta Shringh. He had ignored the dream, whereupon a second time he was ordered to do so. When he had ignored the second warning, a wall of his house collapsed! Taking the divine hint, he set out immediately for Sapta Shringh and was now delivering the statue to "the sadhu." Strange to say, it was from that moment that the ashram really blossomed and grew rapidly. The same statue is in the ashram temple to this day.

In the life of a mahatma there is almost always a period of seeking or tapasya and then a point of breakthrough when the seeker leaps from the pond of selfhood into the sea of universal consciousness, emerging transformed. Once Swamiji pointed to an old photograph of himself and commented, 'That was another Babaji,' pointing to a time before he'd been reborn into God consciousness. It is significant that in 1962 Baba Muktananda sent him a large chair similar to that used by himself and Swami Nityananda. However, Babaji rarely used it and preferred a folded gunny sack on the floor with the children.

Sanyassa

In April 1963, at the express wish of his guru, Laxmi Narayan, who until then had worn the white cloth of a brahmachari, was initiated into the Saraswati order of monks at Kailas Math, Nasik. Swami Akhandananda, the Mahamandeleshwar, himself a great mahatma, spontaneously gave Laxmi Narayan the name Prakashananda (the bliss of the light of awareness) because Laxmi Narayan had become a beacon of his guru's light. From then on, Laxmi Narayan became "Babaji" or "Swamiji."

It had been Baba Muktananda's wish that his disciple, now Swami Prakashananda Saraswati, would assume responsibility for his Ganeshpuri ashram, but Babaji's heart was at Sapta Shringh and he didn't want involvement with the politics and bustle of a large ashram.

For three days Baba pressed me to take the gadi (seat of authority) at his ashram near Ganeshpuri, but I told him, 'A flower garland only has value on account of the flowers; the moment they wither it is thrown away. You are the flowers and I am the string and in the event of your not being present, I would be tossed aside.'

Baba Muktananda finally conceded to Babaji's wish and allowed him to return to Sapta Shringh. However, Babaji promised that as long as his guru was alive, he would make regular visits to the Ganeshpuri ashram, especially in Muktanandaji's absence.

Years later, in May 1982, Baba Muktananda "passed on the gadi" to two young disciples, Swamis Chidivilasananda and Nityananda. The ceremonies consisted of two parts. The first was when Baba was crowned as a spiritual king with a crown and a magnificent red and gold shawl; the second was when, dressed in plain cotton cloth, he gave the throne and kingdom to his two disciples. It is significant that Babaji was present at the ceremonies and was profoundly and movingly honored by his guru, who later lovingly presented him with the same red and gold shawl and a silver-studded stick. It is also interesting that Babaji later gave the same shawl to Swami Pranavananda, an early disciple of Baba Muktananda for whom Babaji had a very special affection and regard. Pranavanandaji, like Babaji, had preferred a quiet, simple life to that of a big ashram. About the silver stick, Babaji later commented, "Baba gave me this stick as authority to point out faults and to speak out if necessary."

Pranavananda's relationship with Babaji was a very special and close one. Pranavananda was a short, round man of infectious vitality and humor who some thought resembled Ganesh, the round-bellied, elephant-headed god who is the remover of all obstacles. Having received sannyas initiation from Baba Muktananda, Pranavanandaji then came and lived with Babaji at Sapta Shringh helping to teach the ashram boys. Soon, however, he left for a solitary life in the wild country at Patana near Chalisgoan where there was an ancient temple to the Mother. In the course of time, he attained great spiritual status and was described by Babaji as a great soul. The unique relationship between the two was visibly manifested as we shall see, and played an important part in both their lives.

Another close disciple is Om Baba, who at present runs the Sapta Shringh Ashram. An ex-military man, he has been engaged in serving the ashram since its conception and it is largely due to his efforts that the ashram has expanded its facilities, such as the ability to offer accommodation to visiting pilgrims. A fine new hostel has also been built for the resident children. Another disciple, Swami Umananda, a gentle man from Karnataka, met Babaji in Sapta Shringh in 1977 and served there for twelve years before moving on.

There is little doubt that Babaji's presence form 1953 to 1980 had an enormous effect in popularizing Sapta Shringh. His universal love, coupled with his atma-jnan, planted the seed of devotion and knowledge in many hearts, both in India and abroad. To be fortunate enough to stay at the ashram with him was an experience to treasure. The effect of his presence on those around him was profound and had the power to awake in a seeker spontaneous faith, devotion, and love, setting doubts at rest. To perceive Babaji as being a physical manifestation of the power of Sapta Shringh was not a difficult matter. On occasion, he would go into seclusion and stay in his hut. Unlike the original hut sixty feet away, this was built nine feet by nine feet by nine feet underground (his meditation cave) in honor of the nine-syllabled Devi mantra he used in his invocation of the Mother. On one such two-day retreat, the entire ashram seemed illuminated and transfigured. Finally, when he appeared on the second day, there was no familiar personality, only a terrifying all-knowing presence. The third day he was back to normal, laughing and joking as usual. There is no doubt that spiritual seekers were able to make fast progress in his presence, as, like his guru, he had the ability to bestow shaktipat. Although not everyone who came to him asked about spiritual matters, nevertheless his knowledge of them was inexhaustible and profound, as was his unassuming wisdom on any subject raised.

One of his chief roles at Sapta Shringh was serving as headmaster in the gurukrula tradition to the ashram students. As one in whom the presence of Jagadamba, the Mother, was active, Babaji's chief function was channeling Her to a confused and troubled world, to transmit Her love to Her children. This he did by oral teaching which spontaneously arose and was never prearranged, and by the presence and shakti he emanated. Although some of the teaching was direct upadesh, a lot of it, as we shall see, was by stories. His storehouse of stories and ability to talk for hours at a time almost amounted to a siddhi, and he was also a great lover of the classical stories such as the Mahabharata and the Ramayana.

Babaji at the Sapta Shringh Ashram

The stories or parables were a unique feature of his teaching. Kirin Narayan wrote a book based around Swamiji's stories, Storytellers, Saints, and Scoundrels.* *He never told a story the same way twice and adapted it to his listeners. Indeed, sometimes he would even name the characters in the story after those sitting in front of him!*

His use of stories was twofold. First, to offer a focus of meditation to his listeners and second, to use the stories to illustrate points to individuals. What struck people most on meeting him was the depth of love which emanated from his being. Quite soon a visitor understood that here was no ordinary sadhu or swami.

Contact with Westerners

During his visits to his guru's Ganeshpuri ashram he had his first major contact with Westerners. However, Babaji, as a traditional sanyasi, was wary of diluting the tradition and teachings handed down through generations with the "freedom" of the West.

Why should I go to America? Here there are stones, trees, and water just like over there. What is so lacking here in India? Here there may be little money, but at least peace can be found. Every place has a quality and no place is alike. Over in America there is money but people lack peace. If I visit there, I'll have to become like that, too. An individual is a little world, and his environment is a big world. Obviously, a man tends to become like his environment. The little world becomes like the big world. A man can become spoiled by that environment. Desire for wealth spoils a man and, even if he desires happiness, it can lead him astray. Anyway, I have a world atlas, and although my eyes are bad, I only have to ask someone to point out a city or a town and that is enough. If I want to see someone, I just close my eyes and envisage them. If I want to talk to them, I talk to

*University of Pennsylvania Press. ISBN 0-8122-819-5

them here (points to his heart). To give a blessing, I can do that just as well from here, even with someone I have never seen before.

In India we have a simple love, whereas in the West the strongest love is for money. If Westerners want to experience our love, it is better for them to come here to India.

In spite of his conviction of the corrupting power of wealth, he loved Westerners as he loved all people, and welcomed his guru's Western disciples who occasionally visited with a care and tenderness that was unforgettable and directly honored his guru:

The respect I am giving you is because you come from my guru. We are all guru-brothers.

Two of the Western seekers Babaji met in the early 1970s are now well-known teachers—Ram Das and Franklin Jones, now known as Avatar Adi Da Samraj. Avatar Adi Da Samraj expressed an interest in this biography and was kind enough to contribute his memories of Swamiji as: ". . .a vessel of happiness. . . .a beautiful being who breathed the spiritual force in such a way that it saturated his entire body. I saw him standing up in a crowd, all of us sitting and only he standing. His entire body was transfigured by white and yellow light all over the body. I was spontaneously moved to bow down to worship this form, this sign. . . .All kinds of people in that room saw Swami Prakashananda transfigured, about one hundred or so. He was the only one who stood up and shone. You cannot do this by an act of will. It was a very sacred occasion. I put my head to the floor to acknowledge That. . . .What a wonder, what beauty. A man that enjoys this sublime state should be remembered. He will be famous in our communion forever."

A third Westerner and less well-known teacher is author and nutritionist Gabriel Cousens, M.D., a family man and holistic physician with all its inherent responsibilities. Dr. Cousens was acknowledged by Babaji on several occasions to be a yogi of real spiritual attainment who "has realized the innate perfection." True to Babaji's agaram bagaram tradition and deeply affected by his contact with Babaji, Dr. Cousens makes no claim to be anything. He functions as a support for people spiritually, as a mentor, and by continuing the tradition of Babaji's work as a lamp from which shaktipat is a vehicle of grace for other lamps to be lit.

Dr. Cousens teaches around the world as well as at the Tree of Life Rejuvenation Center in Patagonia, Arizona, where he is the director.

5

Babaji in Nasik 1980

Babaji's physique testified to tremendous strength and endurance. However, the extreme climate of Sapta Shringh, together with the former years of wandering and tapasya and having been often without adequate food, had taken a heavy toll on his body. A heart condition, high blood pressure, cataracts, and diabetes were only part of the price he paid. It was due mostly to this physical condition that, after 27 years at Sapta Shringh the time finally came for him to leave.

The way in which Babaji finally left Sapta Shringh is interesting. Mr. and Mrs. Khalker had been devotees for some years and had built a bungalow next to the Muktidham, a large temple complex in Nasik about 40 miles south of Sapta Shringh. The bungalow was built partitioned into two. Two rooms for the Khalkers and two for Babaji which he occasionally used. In honor of Babaji's blessing on them it was called "Sadgurukrupa" (blessing of the sadguru).

By the end of 1979, Babaji's health had deteriorated quite badly. This included the complaints already mentioned above. However, it was for cataracts that he went to Bombay to have an operation at the beginning of 1980. While in Bombay recuperating, bad news came from Nasik concerning Mrs. Khalker. Apparently, she was wearing a nylon sari that somehow caught fire while she was cooking. Badly burned, she was now in a hospital. Soon after hearing this news, Babaji was resting on his bed when he felt two invisible hands grasp his feet in a gesture of complete surrender. Almost immediately further news arrived. Mrs. Khalker had died of her burns. Babaji left Bombay and proceeded directly to Nasik. This event was to mark a major transition in his life—the transition from the sublime mountaintop dwelling-place of the Mother to the town, the dwelling-place of Her noisy, rebellious children. He was to remain there until his death.

He now handed the ashram into the care of Om Baba, his disciple since 1955; thereafter, Babaji visited it only on special occasions. It was not an easy transition. People now came in droves like bees to honey to the Khalker's bungalow where he lived. The result was an immediate intensification of Babaji's health crisis. Soaring blood pressure now became his constant companion. Added to this, he went for weeks on a potentially catastrophic fast of black tea and wafer biscuits. This alarming crisis went on until one day he returned from Bombay and announced, 'I think Mrs. Khalker is all right now.'

Something extraordinary had occurred. It appeared that Mrs. Khalker's karma, even in death, had at last been burned away on account of Babaji having taken it upon himself. A message also came from Baba Muktananda, then in America, that he should start eating properly. Finally, he resumed a proper diet, to the intense relief of those around him.

This is a good example of the extraordinary relationship between guru and disciple which extends even beyond death. Here, Babaji's commitment to his disciple overrides his own personal health and even his life.

Daily Life

Babaji's own daily life reflected his wish to spread his guru's message. He would rise at about 3:30 a.m. and take a brief shower, ladling water out of a simple metal bucket. He then spent quite a time in his room in meditation. Visitors would themselves often experience profound meditation states at this time.

If I don't remember God myself and repeat his name, what will I give the people who come here every day?

Afterward, at about 5:30 a.m., he would sit in his reception room to listen to the tape of his guru singing the Guru Gita, an ancient hymn of praise to the guru principle. Anyone who wished to join him was welcome. He had breakfast at 7:00 a.m. Babaji was famous for his love of feeding people and often at "Sadgurukrupa" he would go into the adjoining room where he had his bed and a tiny electric cooker. With a hand inspired by love he would produce wonderful, simple breakfasts for everyone in the room, followed always by hot tea. It was a unique privilege to be present at these occasions. However, Babaji's mood around food was often explosive as he regarded it as a form of God— "Annapurna Brahma", or Food is God. For him, taking food had to be done with the same respect as formal worship and he insisted on absolute reverence toward it. After breakfast he would take a rest in his room and finally emerge at about 10:00 a.m., when people started to arrive to see him. This included the postman who arrived in the morning with letters that were often from abroad, to which he replied as necessary.

The number of people visiting Babaji daily could be sixty or more. These included businessmen, policemen, politicians, farmers, hotel keepers, foreigners of every conceivable nationality, rich and poor. In short, a veritable kaleidoscope of visitors came for advice, spiritual solace, blessings and to hear his stories. Babaji's repertoire of stories seemed limitless and he told them to suit the occasion and the needs of his listeners. With Babaji everything unfolded by the will of God.

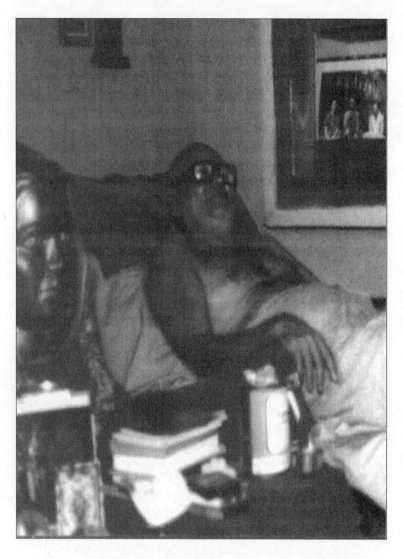

**At the "Shaktidham" in Nasik with
tobacco and "kum kum" close at hand.**

There were no lectures or speeches but rather a spontaneous daily unfolding which was entirely unpredictable except for a general timetable. He took his lunch just after 12:00 p.m. and then rested until 3:00 p.m. For anyone staying with him in the bungalow, often one or two disciples, it was the tradition and sought-after privilege to massage Babaji's legs in his bedroom; this in itself was a profound experience. Babaji's bedroom possessed a deep silence and purity and anyone entering it did well to leave 'his little self' outside. The massage itself was accepted if it was accompanied by real devotion and respect, not necessarily to Babaji as a personality but to the indwelling presence of God. On one occasion an English disciple was massaging him, thinking how special he must be to have this privilege, when one of Babaji's feet whistled through the air missing the Englishman's nose by a fraction of an inch. This happened twice. Finally, the lesson got through. Being a close disciple required continuous alertness and sincerity. Babaji's temperament was unpredictable and sometimes explosive, though always his love and atma-jnan were behind every action and gesture. This fire was the purifying agent which burned away impurities of mind and heart. He often used to say that a disciple should ask the guru for nothing except his abuse as this is what transformed him.

You may wonder why I often abuse those around me! There's a certain insect which, when caught by the wasp and put into the wasp's nest, continually meditates on the sound of the wasp and its sting until finally it becomes a wasp. Similarly, if the guru abuses the disciple, the disciple becomes like his guru by constantly meditating on him.

At 2:30 p.m. Babaji took his tea. Visiting hours were from 3:00 p.m. to 6:00 p.m. At about 5:00 p.m. there would be a "prasad" of a tidbit or sweet to the local children. The last program of the day would be the Shiva Mahimna (hymn to Shiva) at about 7:00 p.m. At about 7:50 p.m. the doors would close and Babaji would often relax listening to the BBC in English, which he said was the only reliable source of news! He loved to lie prone on the floor on one side with head propped up on a cupped hand, listening to it, though how much he understood was never clear. This would be a time of great intimacy and peace. Finally, at 9:00 p.m. he would retire to his room for the night.

How much he slept is uncertain, but usually to sleep in his vicinity was to be kept in a virtually conscious state all night. The power he manifested was tangible and unmistakable. He once said, "Over there the Muktidham, over here the Shaktidham." He was referring to the large temple complex situated about 100 yards from the bungalow called Muktidham, comparing it to his tiny bungalow which he called Shaktidham (abode of Shakti). Babaji had a three-and-one-half foot marble statue of the eighteen-armed Sapta Shringh Devi installed in the tiny room where he met visitors. His important spiritual links were to the Divine Mother in the form of Sapta Shringh, to Dattatreya, and to his guru. On occasions he mentioned that he invoked them in his daily meditations. It is interesting that he kept various articles given to him by his devotees under the mattress of his bed. This was clearly symbolic of his protection and prayers for them.

Babaji's work now consisted almost entirely of seeing people. This included Westerners from Ganeshpuri, most of whom had met Babaji on his visits there. It was in the encounters between him and visitors that most of the teachings and stories which appear later are largely gleaned. However, the real teaching was always nonverbal, a subtle communication which took place from heart to heart.

Mahasamadhi of Baba Muktananda

On the morning of October 3, 1982, there was an urgent knock on Babaji's door at about 3:45 a.m. and a voice of foreboding said, "We have an urgent message from Ganeshpuri." Two men entered

the little room and announced, "Big Maharaj took samadhi (passed
away) last night." The news that his guru had died of a heart attack
during the previous night evoked no dramatic response. On being
questioned on his apparent lack of reaction, Babaji replied with
intense emotion, "How do you know what is in my heart at this
moment?" Babaji quietly packed a bag. By 5:30 a.m. he had left
for Ganeshpuri. Later on, seeing his beloved guru's body, he wept,
but then exclaimed ecstatically, "Baba hasn't left us. He's here."
Baba Muktananda's final teaching, even in death, was the same
message Babaji never tired of proclaiming—the guru is not the body.
Now that the tremendous power, the Guru Principle, which had
animated Baba's body had returned to its universal aspect, the inert
lifeless body was taken in procession, displayed for all to see. It was
Muktananda's last sacrifice and lesson to his devotees. Babaji was
later to say:

We think we are here for ourselves but so do the sheep or goats
that the shepherd keeps. But the shepherd feeds them for his sake, not
for theirs. In the same way, we are here for God's pleasure not for
ours. We all have to go sometime, Rama went, Krishna went. No
matter how great a siddha a person is, he has to go. A body that eats
and defecates—is that the guru? Look at Baba (Muktananda). He had
so many disciples around him, but he was alone when he died.
Nothing could save him either. However, when the Guru Principle
speaks through a mahatma, it can be taken as God's word. Therefore,
the path shown by such a mahatma is eternal. Baba Muktananda was
a great being and his path was great and his message true. His disciples
should meditate on his teaching and spread it.

Health Crisis

In February 1983 an important transition took place. Shortly
after his arrival in Nasik, Babaji had visited Rajhans Hospital and
was examined by Dr. Mohan Rao, the owner of the hospital. The

doctor was astonished to find that Babaji's blood pressure was well over 200 and yet he was apparently unaffected. After treating him, the doctor refused payment but asked for a picture of Babaji's guru instead. "This picture takes a lot of looking after," warned Babaji solemnly. It was the beginning of a profound relationship between the two. Soon afterward the doctor was forced into a life or death emergency operation which he had never performed before and he had hastily consulted Babaji, who said to go ahead. To the doctor's astonishment a pair of hands manifested on the operating table guiding him precisely in the operation. It succeeded and the doctor's journey as a devotee began in earnest.

In March 1983 Babaji went on a long pilgrimage north to Rishikesh, Allahabad, Kanpur, Ayodhya, and Delhi. Two days after his return to Nasik he fell so severely ill that he was admitted to Rajhans Hospital. For two days his life seemed to hang on a thread and he instructed that his "close people" should be told of his condition. They came from far and wide. Indeed, even Swami Pranavananda, who was spending the summer months near Dehra Dun, drove four days through temperatures of more than 100 degrees to tend to Babaji. From morning to evening Pranavanandaji looked after him tirelessly and devotedly and gradually Babaji's condition improved. "Certainly I was to have gone, but the Lord has recalled my ticket," he laughed. "It seems that because I am ready for death every moment, he (death) is avoiding me." He added that he had come so close to death that he had the direct experience of seeing the cosmic cycle of souls "lined up" to be born as well as seeing them come out of embodied existence.

It was in 1983 that on the invitation of the doctor and his wife that Babaji moved into a room adjoining the hospital. His health had reached a point where it required constant monitoring and this the doctor and his wife, who was also a doctor, did with tremendous dedication, on occasion staying up all night with Babaji.

This was the beginning of the final stage of Babaji's life. Apart from occasional visits, such as to Swami Pranavananda's ashram *and day trips to Sapta Shringh, he rarely left the three-room apartment adjoining the hospital. However, there was one pleasant and delightful interlude which came at the end of 1984.*

Australia

For some years there had been standing offers for Babaji to go abroad. These especially came from Dr. Gabriel Cousens in America and from Mrs. Joan Halpern of Perth, Australia. Finally, in December of 1984, he agreed to visit Perth, where he spent six weeks as Mrs. Halpern's guest, accompanied by three others, including Dr. Mohan Rao. He made several conditions: no advertising of his presence and no lectures. However, his simplicity, love, and presence did not take long to make themselves felt. Soon a good number of people came morning and afternoon to breathe the rarefied air of a great man of God. It was a quiet, gentle visit which Babaji seemed to enjoy. A preliminary hitch to the visit had been Babaji's passport application in which he had written the name of his father as Swami Muktananda Paramahamsa. This had been queried. "If they don't want to give me the passport, that's fine. A sadhu's father is his guru, he has no other," he said.

After the return from Australia, Babaji's movements grew very restricted and he became more confined to his rooms adjoining Rajhans Hospital. He now rarely traveled.

His timetable, however, continued as before. He rose at 3:30 a.m. and the day consisted of the Guru Gita *programs followed by visiting hours in the morning and afternoon. Around 5:00 p.m. there was a children's program attended by up to fifty children from the locality. The* bhajan *was led by Dr. Mohan Rao and* prasad *and sometimes clothing was handed out by Babaji.*

A great and special joy was when Swami Pranavananda invited him to his ashram on special festival occasions. Since arriving in Patana, Swamiji had transformed the isolated Devi *temple into a place of devotion where, on occasions, thousands of devotees*

51

Near Perth, Australia

gathered. By 1987, Pranavanandaji's reputation had spread all over India and his devotees included many high-ranking government officials.

Perhaps the most special occasion was when the Palki, a statue of the Sapta Shringh Devi, was brought in procession to meet her sister Devi at Patana, in a special palanquin. This took two or three days on foot and when at last on the great day the palanquin arrived at Patana, Babaji and Swami Pranavananda would meet it. It was a very touching and moving moment. The meeting of the two "sisters" was made even more poignant by the presence of the two great swamis who had surrendered everything to the Divine Mother. There was a delightful equality and love between the two which was unmistakable, and Babaji clearly approved of Pranavanandaji as a beloved son who had won the keys to his father's house.

The palki's arrival in Patana was accompanied by exuberance and celebrations on a lavish scale. Literally thousands of people were fed from open-air kitchens producing mountains of rice and other edibles.

Swami Pranavananda: A "Great Soul."

6

Mahasamadhi 1988

It was in 1987 that Pranavanandaji made a request of Babaji, with the mischievous glint of humor that characterized him, that intuitively he must have known to be relevant in the near future. It concerned Babaji's frequently stated wish to be given jal samadhi on his death. He had given instructions for his body to be transported to the Narmada River in Gujerat and "given to the fish." Pranavanandaji had other ideas.

"Maharaj, now of course your body is yours, but after your death surely it won't be any longer! Therefore, let us take care of your body and do with it what we feel we should. I myself promise to do whatever traditional ritual requires. Allow us to inter your body in Sapta Shringh, in the meditation cave under your hut!" This request was made with such love and humor that Babaji agreed to it.

The indifferent health that dogged Babaji so interminably persisted relentlessly right into 1988. However, early in that year, an invitation to Babaji came from Swami Pranavananda to come to the inauguration of Kali Math, a temple Pranavandaji had built and dedicated to Mother Kali. Babaji went and returned after several happy days with Pranavanandaji. He was radiant. It was as if the Mother wanted to give Her son a final benediction before accepting him back to Herself in eternity. It was to mark the last chapter of his life.

It seemed to those close to him that Babaji had gained a new lease on life. His health suddenly improved and his mood was expansive and full of familiar dynamism and joy. This continued right until June 10, 1988. There was no warning of what was to occur.

It was Babaji's custom to sit with the children for the evening bhajan program in the evening and the tenth of June was no exception. After handing out the usual prasad, he retired to his room but soon afterward was afflicted with severe chest pains. This was nothing unusual for someone with intermittent angina. However, this was something much more—a major heart attack. Babaji calmly told Dr. Mohan Rao and his wife, who rushed to his side, "There's nothing anyone can do for me now."

The soul of a great man of God at last found release from the tired, afflicted body. He was gone.

The next morning, Babaji's body was taken home to his beloved Sapta Shringh and then taken in procession to the room which had been his abode for so many years. The meditation room under his bed had been hastily excavated during the night and the body was interred in the presence of Swami Pranavananda, who, as promised, supervised the proceedings.

Many others were present, including Om Baba, Swami Umananda, Swami Krishnananda, and Madhav Chaitanya. Certain disciples had intuited Babaji's death and one of his close disciples had started out for Nasik from North India even before the evening of June 10, 1988.

The main and final ritual came in Sapta Shringh sixteen days later on June 27, 1988. It was attended by hundreds, including Swami Vidyananda, the Mahamandaleshwar of the Saraswati *order of monks, Swami Pranavananda, Om Baba, and others. The following account of the ritual was written by an English eyewitness, and gives some idea of the atmosphere.*

"*The eve of June 27. Cooking all night and people start to pour in. Om Baba and Swami Umananda both tireless and self-giving. In constant movement and preparation, giving orders, meeting the people who have come from far and wide to honor Babaji one last time. Yes, probably never again will we all be here together like this. Our final salute to a man who had loved us all unconditionally. But was it our final salute? No way. Our lives will be tinged with his presence, teachings, abuse, love! We will be, all of us to some extent, his lights.*

"*Finally, Sunday dawns and they are all there. The familiar faces too numerous to mention. The Mahamandaleshwar (Swami Vidyananda), Pranavanandaji, Om Baba, the Collector (Chief Administrator of Nasik District), sadhus, some with matted locks, some smeared with ash, and several sannyasis. And the devotees came, from Bombay, Nasik, and all over. Faces so familiar. The exchanged look of joy and recognition, the hugs, the tears. The open-air program starts at about 8:00 a.m. and gradually the chant builds up: 'Om namo Bhagavate Prakashanandaya' (I bow to God in the form of light). Yes, everyone starts to feel it. Babaji's gone to God, he is universal now, always with you. Suddenly an old man leaps up and starts dancing and singing, leading us. He has forgotten himself and it catches like fire. Then Vidyanandaji starts singing, beautifully. The rain comes down and the tarpaulin is not big enough. Someone holds a leaking umbrella over him. Then Vidyananda starts talking. He is inspired, authoritative, humorous, and totally at ease. He obviously loves Babaji.*

'*Are you sad?' Vidyananda cajoles, 'Don't you understand that Prakashanandaji has merged back into his Source? Is that a cause for weeping or for joy?'*

'*For joy!' replies every heart.*

"When the speech was finished there was a great feeling of openness to the Guru Principle which Babaji embodied. The last event I witnessed was the bhojan prasad (special meal) in which several thousand people were fed. Before leaving, I took the liberty of presenting a flower garland and coconut on behalf of all those Westerners who could not be there in person."

•   •   •

The meditation room which had so many times witnessed Babaji's communion with the Divine had now become his Samadhi Shrine (a shrine built over the burial place of a saint). Today, a fine structure towers over the site of the original 9' x 9' x 9' hut. The splendor of his Samadhi Shrine represents the love of all those for whom he is alive today.

PART II

TEACHINGS AND PARABLES

"You should note down what comes out of this mouth because one day many people will benefit from it."

The teachings contained in Part II were compiled at Babaji's specific suggestion over a period of time during his meetings with a wide variety of visitors. They were always spontaneous utterances made to individuals in specific contexts and situations. It is hoped that the heart of the reader will recognize and extract what is useful and life-giving rather than taking each statement as general advice.

One of Babaji's favorite teaching mediums was parables, or fables. For him a story was not something fixed or rigid and he was a master at adapting it to the needs of his listeners, or perhaps to an individual. The stories were never told quite the same way twice. They served to consolidate a teaching as well as providing a single authentic focus of attention for his listeners, who each interpreted them according to his or her understanding.

This collection of teachings and parables has been compiled over a period of eight years of being in daily contact with Babaji and an attempt has been made to put them into a logical order and framework under specific headings, as well as to cover the main *aspects of his teachings. As in Part I, the author's words are italicized, all standard text is Swamiji's words unless otherwise stated, and any Sanskrit words appearing for the first time are italicized.*

Religious teachings are the crumbs left on the table after the great **satpurushas** have dined and left their bodies to return to God.

Real knowledge of God cannot be had just through written teachings which can be likened to crumbs compared to the bread of life which is God Himself. This bread or feast can only be granted by a direct contact or meeting between the individual Soul (Jivatma) and the Universal Soul (Paramatma). The jnani is a mirror of the Paramatma and facilitates this direct perception in the hearts of those he meets. Although in a sense this book can be no more than the crumbs left over after the feast, nevertheless, words have great power; especially the words of a jnani, which are imbued with the power of the Supreme Self, of the Guru Principle (Guru Tatva). The nature of the Guru Principle may be said to be the central pillar of Babaji's teaching.

Guru Tattva

"The Guru is the Eternal Principle."

Who then is the guide of a seeker wishing to make the journey back to the source of his existence? Who is the guru or true teacher?

The syllable gu means maya or ignorance and the syllable ru is that which destroys it. The Guru Tattva (guru principle) dwells in the heart of a human being, not in the physical heart, but in the spiritual heart at the source of the mind, shining like a pure crystal. He is known as the **angustha purusha**, the thumb-sized person.

This is a lake. (Babaji describes a circle with his hand.) One man took out a little water and put it aside, calling it Christianity. Another man came, took some water and called it Islam, another Buddhism, and so on. But whether we are Buddhist, Christian, or Hindu, the Guru Principle is one. Many people ignorantly think it is represented by one particular, unique manifestation or person and that surrender means to give everything to that one. No! True surrender does not mean to give everything to an individual but to God, who dwells within us as the Guru Principle.

It is always the disciples of a great jnani who try to get members for their 'party.' The founders of the great religions have eaten the real spiritual food and gone back to God. The disciples show the world an empty plate with a few crumbs and say, 'Here, eat this.' From the point of view of God and the jnani, differences like Christian, Muslim, and Jain don't exist. Actually, all mahatmas say the same thing and needlessly people fight over different interpretations of one truth.

> *For Babaji, therefore, the distinctions of religion, creed, and class were purely manmade, as one God pervaded them all. One day a Hindu lady visiting Babaji complained that her husband had lost his job.*

Go to the nearby *durgah*. Having offered food to the Muslim saint, then distribute it as prasad to any visitors and children who happen to be visiting the durgah. You should mentally ask the saint to grant your desire and make him a promise to be fulfilled after your desire is accomplished. All saints belong to one God.

> *Once an Australian confessed that he had visited many teachers and mahatmas but was unsure who his guru really was.*

The guru is you yourself in the form of the indwelling atma. It is this atma which gives the world its existence. If you give your allegiance to this body, for example, (pointing to himself), you are making a mistake. All bodies, even the great Siddhas, have to go. Look at Ram, Krishna, and Jesus. They all had to go one day. No, the Guru is the Eternal Principle. Know and serve *that* Guru and don't get burned by the fire of wrong understanding.

> *This message was delivered with such power and conviction that the Australian's confusion fell away and was replaced by joy.*
> *As one who had no interest in attracting either disciples or an organization, Babaji often found himself in the position of helping*

seekers break through identification with a particular form. Once an advanced American seeker, a well-known doctor and healer, came to Babaji. He was in considerable conflict because his spiritual understanding had grown beyond the concept of serving and identifying the guru as one particular individual. At the same time, he acknowledged that the tremendous expansion of spiritual consciousness he had experienced had been due to contact with this teacher. Babaji told him:

Actually, it is the Guru Principle dwelling within you that does everything. Did it not make you aware of the need for a guru in the first place? Did it not lead you to him? Was it not this indwelling principle which was ignited as a result? The Guru Principle is the real doer.

Babaji, therefore, never lost an opportunity to stress the importance of not confusing the Guru Principle with a particular physical form. It seems that even great devotees have to learn this lesson.

To wean Hanuman away from attachment to his physical form, Ram dropped his ring into the ocean. Hanuman, the perfect devotee, immediately dived down to retrieve it but on reaching the ocean bed, found not one, but hundreds of similar rings.

"Which is Ram's," he asked a passing fish.

"They're all his," came the reply. "Don't you know how many Rams there have been throughout infinite time?"

A jnani or mahatma is, therefore, one in whom the Guru Principle is active and blazing. When a great Soul reaches such a stage of transparency that he can be an agent or vehicle for the Guru Principle, he receives an order either from his guru or from the Guru Principle itself to serve the function of guru, or teacher.

"All saints belong to one God."

8

The Guru

"When the Guru Principle speaks through the vehicle of a true mahatma, it can be taken as God's word."

Babaji never proclaimed or appointed himself as a Guru or teacher. Nevertheless, hundreds of people regarded him as a Guru although he himself was careful not to display his spiritual status and deliberately remained "agaram bagaram."

When you value something greatly, you will protect it by keeping it hidden carefully away. Spiritual things should not be put on display.

Only on very rare occasions did he acknowledge his attainment. Once a close disciple who had served Babaji over an extended time was massaging his legs. "Have you ever examined the soles of my feet?" asked Babaji suddenly. Surprised, the disciple confessed he hadn't. Whereupon Babaji pointed out certain unique marks similar to those on his guru's feet. "Just keep serving me. You need do nothing else," advised Babaji.

His attainment and authority sprang from two sources. First, as we have seen, from the spiritual realization earned by years of intense sadhana and tapasya; second, from his spiritual lineage. We have seen that Babaji was first and foremost a son of the Mother as she appears in the form of the Sapta Shringh Devi. We have already seen Sapta Shringh Devi to be intimately connected with siddha vidya and the "Nath" lineage. The tradition of Siddha Yoga is also alive in the more recent succession from Bhagavan Nityananda to his disciple Swami Muktananda, and thence to Swami Chidvilasananda, the disciple of Muktanandaji, who is the present head of Gurudev Siddha Peeth Ashram in the state of Maharashta and to Swami Nityananda. We have already seen Baba Muktananda's recognition of Babaji on two main occasions. First, in sending a large teacher's chair to Sapta Shringh in 1962, and second, in requesting Babaji to "sit on the gadi" of his ashram. His teachings were, therefore, imbued with the power of his spiritual lineage as well as the conviction of his own spiritual realization.

To attain liberation, firstly you should follow the suggestions and disciplines of your guru. Secondly, learn to have the awareness that you are not the doer. Consider all your thoughts and actions to have their source in God, not in 'you.' Don't think of the body—the eyes, ears, and hands as yours. Rather, see them as instruments through which God acts. Liberation means to see everything as existing in God: the same One dwells in everything and everyone.

The work of the guru is essentially that. To ensure that his disciple reaches the ocean of God. This he does by various means— by oral teaching, but mainly by igniting the heart of the disciple with his own lighted candle. Thus he leads the aspirant to the Guru within his own heart and frees him from all dependence on external objects, ideas, philosophies and creeds. Finally, the Guru frees the disciple from dependence on himself. The mystery of the Guru, who is both formless and yet with form, is the mystery of God Himself.

Despite warnings about limiting the Guru to a particular form, nevertheless, Babaji was emphatic about the need for a guru as one who can lead the aspirant to recognition of the truth. Once an American visitor came to Babaji with this very question in her mind, of whether she needed a guide and whether Babaji himself could show her the way to God. Before she even spoke, he began a story.

Tulsidas and Hanuman

Before Tulsidas became the great saint he was later to become, he lived for some time at Chitrakut, where *Rama* and *Sita* had lived, in order to realize God in the form of Rama, his *Ishta devata* or family deity. In fact, he had little idea of how to go about realizing his aim when a nature spirit took pity on him and told him, 'Look, to approach Rama, you have to go through Hanuman.'

But where to find Hanuman? The answer came that a certain Brahmin living in a nearby village recites the *Ramayana* every day which many people attend, including Hanuman himself. The latter takes the form of an old man and always waits after the recitation until everyone has gone.

So Tulsidas duly attended the recitation and true enough there was the old man. When everyone had left at the end, Tulsidas bowed to the old gentleman.

'I know you are really Hanuman. Please help me!' he cried. Moved by Tulsidas's passionate appeal regarding obtaining darshan of Lord Rama, Hanuman graciously answered, 'Hold a feast in the village and I'll invite Rama to come.'

Tulsidas, with trembling anticipation, made all arrangements for a feast (Bandhara) the following day, inviting the Brahmins and dignitaries. However, no sign of Ram! To add insult to injury, a dog appeared at the end and started licking the scraps. Furious, the Brahmins grabbed their sticks and the dog ran off.

The next day a bitterly disappointed Tulsidas again approached Hanuman in the form of the old man and reproachfully demanded why Rama had not come to the feast.

'You fool, don't you realize Rama came in the form of that dog you chased away? Didn't you recognize him? Now you will have to give another bandara.'

Again, Tulsidas carefully made arrangements and put on a more splendid feast than before. But again no sign of Ram or even the dog. The final insult was when two 'untouchables' came at the end and tried to sit down near the Brahmins. Livid with rage the Brahmins reached for their sticks, cursing, to chase them off. Tulsidas, feeling cheated and very disgruntled, approached the old man the next day at the recitation. As soon as they were alone, Hanuman started severely scolding Tulsidas.

'Can't you understand anything, you imbecile?" he demanded. "Ram and Sita both came to your feast in the form of those two untouchables and even then you did not recognize them.'

At last Tulsidas' pride broke down and he wept bitterly.

'I am so foolish and ignorant! The only way I will ever recognize God is if he comes in the form of the Rama with which I am familiar.'

Seeing his inability to recognize God's manifestations, Hanuman agreed to invite Rama again on condition that Tulsidas invite the entire village, including children, untouchables, and animals. So Tulsidas prepared a magnificent feast to which everyone was invited and sure enough, Rama, Sita, and Laxman came in person.

> *Babaji's final comment to the American visitor, made with a smile, was as follows.*

So, grab on to the feet of that old man and don't let go!

> *His meaning as to whom the old man referred in this case was evident.*
>
> *The feet of a jnani have a great significance in the Indian tradition as the point of access to his spiritual power. A Canadian*

describes his chance meeting with Swamiji in a street in a small Maharasthra pilgrim town in 1973 as follows. "*My eyes were on the road in front of me when I glimpsed a pair of feet coming toward me down the far side of the depression. At the moment that the feet came into sight at a distance of about fifty feet, a powerful rush of energy came up from the ground through my own feet and body and lifted my head and flooded my mind with light and joy. I found myself looking into the eyes of a large, smiling sanyassi. I saluted him and passed on. Later I learned that the swami was called Prakashananda.*"

9

Guru and Disciple

*"The seed received from the Sadguru, if nourished
by the water of spiritual Sadhana, will one
day blossom into self-realization."*

*The guru's main work is to offer a path (marg) to God—a
Sadhana. This will inevitably be based on those seed principles and
disciplines which have guided his own path to God realization. The
guru-disciple relationship in some form is crucial to the spiritual
path. It generally begins with some form of subtle transmission in
which the power of the teacher and his lineage is experienced in the
disciple's inner being. This transmission of spiritual consciousness
is like planting a seed.*

Initiation

Look at a coconut. A young coconut has fluid and thin flesh. Put
it in the ground and no tree will emerge as it is immature. But plant
a mature coconut whose flesh has hardened and it will produce a tree.
Similarly, we have to become mature in order to produce spiritual
fruit. If you take an unripe mango seed and plant it similarly nothing

will happen, no matter how much you water it. However, a ripe seed, if tended, will grow into a vast tree which itself contains seeds. Each of these has the potential to itself become a mango tree. Likewise, the seed in the form of mantra received from the sadguru, if nourished by the water of spiritual sadhana, will one day blossom into self-realization and the disciple, in his turn, will be able to pass on the same ripe seed to others. This is the meaning of 'jyota se jyota—one lighted candle can light many others.' However, whereas the guru's light has this power and does not get depleted, the disciple has to beware the wind of egotism which may extinguish his lighted wick. For this reason the guru puts a protective glass around the disciple.

Babaji takes a box of matches and removes a match.

Within this match is potential fire but only when it contacts a matchbox does ignition take place. Likewise, within the disciple is hidden the sleeping kundalini shakti. However, contact with the Sadguru is necessary to awaken it. Here is another example. If there is well water below the ground, to start the water flowing up a pipe, we have to take water from above and pour it down the pipe until it meets the well water below. Only then will the well water start flowing, needing no further outside assistance. In the same way, once the kundalini shakti is awakened through contact with the Sadguru, spiritual unfoldment will occur spontaneously and automatically within the disciple. Once the disciple's identification with the body is burned up by the awakened shakti, he is free or liberated.

Hidden within milk is *ghee* but to extract it we have to churn the cream until we get butter. From butter we can then separate the ghee. Similarly, hidden in the mind is the pure atma and to separate the two we churn the mind by repeating the guru mantra until the "ghee" of the atma gets separated from the mind. This stage is called atma jnan and when the disciple reaches it in his sadhana, his atma jyoti finally gains the same power as his guru, of being able to light other candles without itself becoming depleted. There is no true knowledge without the guru. Therefore, earn a little knowledge because it will attract more knowledge to itself. Similarly, earn love and it will attract more love to itself. Knowledge flows to knowledge and love flows to love.

Need for the Guru

Namdev and Vitoba Khechar

Namdev was a great devotee of Lord Vithal (Krishna) and indeed used to talk with him as one friend to another. Naturally, he was extremely proud of the fact and, unknown to him, the devil of pride worked into his heart until he was far from the true spiritual knowledge of God. So one day God, who knows all things, took a hand in the proceedings.

The devotees of *Pandharapur* were gathered together as usual for their devotions and afterward the great saint Jnaneshwar Maharaj told Gora the potter to go around the assembled company, which included Namdev, in order to "test the pots." So Gora duly went from one devotee to another tapping each "pot" (head) and pronouncing whether they were spiritually mature or not! At last he came to Namdev, and tapping his head he pronounced, 'This one is unripe!'

It was agreed by one and all he was in need of a guru. Furious and thoroughly humiliated, Namdev went straight home and complained to Lord Vithal, who was less sympathetic than Namdev should have liked. Gently, Lord Vithal suggested that the scriptures were doubtless correct in stipulating the necessity of a guru for true knowledge of God. The Lord then suggested that Namdev should go to a certain Shiva temple where a great saint was staying and beg for instruction.

Dejected and sullen, Namdev set off and upon entering the Shiva temple was horrified to see an old man apparently asleep with his feet resting on the *lingam*. Such sacrilege was too much for Namdev. Shaking the old man to wake him up, Namdev seized his legs from off the lingam and placed them down. Wonder of wonders, as soon as the feet touched the ground, another lingam rose up to support them. Again he moved the feet and another lingam rose out of the ground! The old man at last opened his eyes and said, 'Why are you bothering an old man? Tell me, is there anyplace which doesn't belong to God? Is there any form which is not his?'

At these words Namdev's eyes were opened and the pride and limitation of his unique friendship with Lord Vithal evaporated forever. With tears pouring down his cheeks he clutched the old man's feet in thanks of joy. He'd at last found his guru.

> *In the same way, people meeting Babaji for the first time soon understood that here was a teacher, a guru, whose presence and words had the power to transform a person, and to confer a wide cosmic vista against which his listeners' burdens and anxieties seemed to pale into relative insignificance. Sometimes, if he felt his visitors were open to hearing it, he expounded what he called 'my philosophy'—his viewpoint on the nature of reality, creation, and man's part in it.*

10

Brahman—The Origin

"The manifest and the unmanifest are really one."

Originally in the beginning, there was No–thing. Infinitude. Supreme Brahman (Shiva), birthless and deathless. And yet within that no–thing was some–thing. That some–thing can be called Shakti, vibration, or Nada. To understand Brahman from which this whole universe had emerged, you need Shakti, its dynamic aspect sometimes called Devi or Bhagwati, the Divine Mother. They are like the two sides of a single coin. The Principle of Shiva-Shakti is, in fact, neither male nor female. It is eternal and beyond understanding and all created things. It is God. Even the scriptures are powerless to approach that, saying helplessly, 'neti neti' (not this, not this). Shiva is the unmanifest, No–thing in which All–things are potential. Shakti is the manifest, the Some–thing within No–thing. Actually, the manifest and the unmanifest are really one, they only appear different. If you put a stick in front of you, you can talk of left and right, but remove the stick and where is left and right?

Actually, man and woman are not made for each other as they might think, but are made for Him. One Brahman becomes two. To create a current you need two wires and both are equally important. It is only our limited vision which sees a difference between man and woman.

Though Shiva and Shakti are beyond the senses and mind and cannot be seen, they can be intuited by the spiritual eye of knowledge. For example, you cannot see the government, but by observing its various manifestations and forms such as laws, rules, and its representatives, we can understand something of the government itself. Similarly, by looking at the manifestation or creation of Brahman, we come to understand something of It.

Look at this tube light here, (pointing above his head). When electricity flows into it, it manifests light. Similarly, when electricity flows into a fridge or heater, we get cold and heat, respectively. But is electricity itself light, cold, or heat? No. All we know is when we touch it we get a shock! One thing is certain. Two wires are needed for it to work, negative and positive. One wire is not enough. Similarly, creation is manifested through the principle of Shiva and His creative power, Shakti. Shakti is in all beings and in all things. Dead wood may look inert and you will probably say contains no Shakti, but rub two pieces together and you have fire. The blaze arising from that tiny spark could set the whole world ablaze.

From Shakti first the element of ether or space (akash) comes into existence, and its quality or emanation is sound or nada. Ether gives rise to air or wind, which has two qualities, touch and sound. The friction of wind gives rise to fire, which has three qualities, touch, sound, and vision (it can also be seen). With the interaction of these three elements, space, air, and fire, emerges the fourth element, water. This has four qualities, touch, vision, sound, and taste. When these four elements interact, earth comes into being, which contains five qualities, including smell. These five great elements are the building blocks of creation. Indeed, man's body is thus composed and when the soul or atma comes to dwell in it, a human being is the result.

However, being and intelligence is not confined to human beings. Plants also have intelligence and communicate to one another, as do birds. We just do not understand their language. Does not a police dog have intellect? It can be trained to catch a criminal in a way no policeman can. Indeed, if you look at animals and birds, you find that in certain ways they manifest more intelligence than human beings. See how dogs and other animals mate only in season, whereas man's sexual appetite goes unchecked. Look how birds migrate for thousands of miles to a particular spot and how an animal can find its way home when let loose far from its home. Think what service trees do for the world! They combat pollution by giving out clean oxygen and their branches give shade from the sun and a shelter and refuge to man, animals, and insects. The bark and leaves of certain trees are used for medicine. Others produce flowers and fruits. Think of the peace and joy given by flowers. Even in death a tree is invaluable and its wood sold for many purposes—cooking, making furniture, and even building houses. Nothing is wasted. What service for the world!

As for animals, after death their meat is bought for high prices for food and their skins become leather which then becomes belts, shoes, and the like. Even the animal's gut can be used in making various racquets for sports. The fur of certain animals is also highly prized and even the bones are crushed and used as fertilizer.

For all life forms, however, there is a guarantee, just like a watch. For example, a certain kind of flea is born, married, has children, and dies, all within the space of a few hours. A man's life span is up to 120 years, as is an elephant's, whereas a dog's life span is only about twelve years. Certain trees and plants live for only a few months, some a few years, and some for hundreds of years. All the various species, however, are dependent on food to sustain them.

Actually, even the bodies of life forms do not get destroyed after death but only change their form. For example, the crushed bones of an animal used for fertilizer come up in the form of a plant. The plant is then eaten and passed out of the system into the earth, and so the cycle goes on. Tell me, does anything really get destroyed?

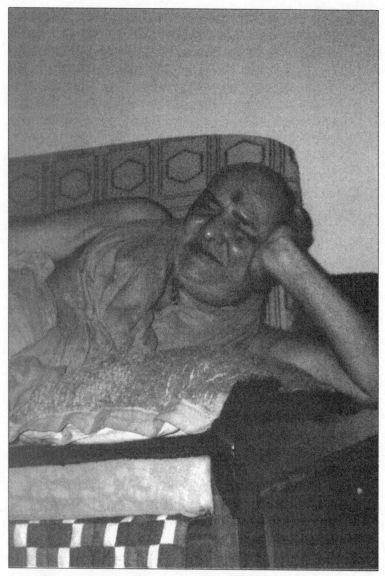

"Look there, inside. If you look outside of yourself, you won't find anything."

11

The Human Being

"A human being can acquire
God-like qualities and uplift humanity."

So what of Man? In the same way that a cloth consists of many individual strands to which it owes its strength, we also consist of many lives. We think of ourselves as one life but actually this body consists of many organisms.

This body is a world, a universe just like the one outside and that is why Satpurushas all say to look there, inside. If you look outside of yourself, you won't find anything.

In this body are seven seas, such as ghee (fat) a red sea (blood), a salt sea (urine), a sea of acid (stomach), and so on. [Babaji points to his head.] This is a hill with forest growing (hair). If not maintained carefully, all kinds of creatures will make their homes there. There are mountain ranges [points to two arms and two legs]. Between them in the valley is jungle with flowing rivers. Different animals and birds come and inhabit this world of the body and try to cultivate fields (ringworm, etc.) and establish territories (the various diseases). A mosquito tells its children 'I'll bring you food' and then goes to drill for blood on this world. I, as the owner or God, protect my territory by killing the mosquito. Similarly, by use of medicines I attempt to wipe out the alien organisms causing me dis-ease.

Let us suppose a great swami or mahatma dies unattended somewhere. Within three days a terrible smell will emanate from his body and there will be a danger of infection from cholera. A doctor might have to be called in to inoculate any local residents and a dog eating his flesh might even suffer madness. Certainly the great Mahatma's body will have to be burried or burnt immediately. And yet, in the scriptures it is said that to be given the body of a human being is the choicest of births.

What then is so special about a human being? It is man who has access to three higher faculties that separate him from the animal kingdom. Jnan (knowledge), Vijnan (higher spiritual knowledge), and finally, the experience of Anand (supreme bliss). These faculties grant him the unique capacity to realize that his source is God and the ability to return to Him. But what is it that has its eternal source in God? Certainly not the body.

The scriptures talk of the angustha purusha (thumb-sized person) which dwells in the heart. Within it are contained all the stored desires and deeds of the individual soul. This angustha purusha uses the body and manifests through it. When its play in a particular body is finished, the body is discarded and the soul finds a new vehicle through which to manifest. Some people say there is no reincarnation but it is a fact nevertheless that we take birth according to our deeds. Whatever role destiny has given us to perform, we will have to play out to the end.

As we can see in the following story, happiness lies in accepting our particular destiny as part of God's leela or divine play.

Everything's for the Best

A certain king one day had an accident in which his toe had to be amputated. Seeing the misfortune, his favorite minister remarked in the presence of the suffering king, 'Very good, everything's for the best.' On hearing this, the king became furious and dismissed him on the spot from his position as Chief Minister. To the king's astonishment, the minister's reply was, 'Very well. Everything's for the best.'

Some little time later the king went out hunting in a dense jungle as was his habit and whilst chasing a deer somehow got separated from his companions and became hopelessly lost. Now there lived in that jungle a primitive tribe who habitually offered human sacrifice to their god. A party of them cunningly succeeded in capturing the king. Binding him hand and foot, they took him to their village and threw him in a dark hut. Soon the full moon day came and the villagers were dancing in frenzied anticipation for the moment when their victim was to be sacrificed.

At last the high priest, in a trance and brandishing a big sword, ordered the prisoner to be brought out; the king was garlanded and brought in front of the deity. Suddenly the priest stiffened. 'Why did you bring him? He is incomplete. He has already been cut,' he shouted disgustedly, pointing to the king's severed toe. 'Get him out of here.'

So, a couple of days later, the chastened king limped back to his capital. Despite his condition, he summoned his former minister and told his story.

'Beloved friend, my amputated toe has saved my life. You were absolutely correct in saying "very good" and I request you humbly to accept back your former position as my Chief Minister. But tell me, why did you also say about your dismissal, "Very well, everything's for the best." '

'Your Majesty,' replied the minister, 'everything happens for the best. Look at it this way. If you hadn't dismissed me, I would most certainly, as your Chief Minister, have been caught along with you by those tribesmen. Whereas they rejected you as a sacrifice, it is doubtful they would have rejected me!'

In fact, it is our destiny that we come into the world to act out like actors in a drama. Actually, I'm not a Swami and he [Babaji points to a visitor] is not a doctor. It's the atma which assumes these various roles for its own satisfaction and sport.

In a man not only are the five elements present, but additional faculties necessary for the soul's play in the body. These are manas, buddhi, and ahamkara. Together they constitute what we commonly call mind or antahkarana (the inner psychic instrument). They are, in effect, the eyes of the soul.

12

Mind—Manas, Buddhi, Ahamkara

*"The one who has understood
this world is always happy."*

Manas is the faculty to understand and cognize, though it has the ability and tendency to wander off on its own, like an independent entity. It is, however, the servant of the soul (atma) and totally dependent on it. Nevertheless, without this faculty there could be no cognition of the external world.

Buddhi is the faculty of intellect and is a sort of personal assistant to the soul. Connected to manas, it can find out from the storehouse of the mind (chitta—memories, etc.) about past events.

Now look at me. Two eyes [Babaji raises his fingers and taps his glasses] a nose, ears. Your mind is resting on this body and the atma accompanies it. Without it there can be no seeing. The mind sees and reports back to the individual soul through means of the intellect which says, 'It's Prakashananda.'

It's the same with listening. What hears is not the ears, but the atma, which then consults with the intellect in order to sort out information heard. The intellect is like a storehouse and manas like a honey bee which travels from flower to flower collecting honey to place in it. For whom? Inside is the Queen Bee and it is for her that the bee darts back and forth. She is the soul (jivatma) and when she wants honey she can find it in the storeroom, the intellect.

The faculty of discrimination is also in the intellect because manas collects and brings whatever it can find, good and bad. It is the intellect which sorts out the information using discrimination: this is good, this is bad. Therefore, discrimination lies in the intellect (buddhi), not in the manas. Think this over carefully. If someone says they lack peace, they are referring to the intellect and if the intellect develops a fault, the result is what the world calls madness.

The Creator of Division

Ahamkara is the idea within the mind of being a separate entity— the concept of yours and mine, my house, my wife, my body. For a small baby everything is the same. He cannot recognize his mother and father. Then he eats, grows, and gains strength. As he grows, his illusions also grow: these are my parents, my brother, my clothes, my honor, my knowledge. The sense of 'I' produces these illusions. Actually, everything is the Lord's. From this same ego emanates what we call the world with its division of nationality, creed, philosophy, virtue and sin, pleasure and pain. It is the I who chooses its friends, enemies, guru, and its God. What actually is this I, and what is its source? We should inquire into it in order to find the truth. It was for this reason Baba (Muktananda) used to say 'Meditate on your Self, understand your Self. God dwells within you as you.'

Actually, without the I of individuality the concept of the world would vanish. The truth is that the Ahamkara or ego is illusory. We are not separate from Universal Consciousness. The little I identified with the body is the troublemaker. The true I, however, is the Aham of Krishna when he says in the Bhagavad Gita 'I am in all things and pervade everywhere.' Similarly, when Jesus says, 'No man comes to the Father by Me,' he isn't talking of Me as a particular body or personality, but of HAM, the universal I.

84

However, it is through this very vehicle of ego that a man returns to God. Between sun and nature is space. Nature is a product of the sun's rays and depends upon their warmth and light entirely for its existence. Similarly, the little I has no existence of its own outside the Universal I. From one comes many and from many comes one. First there is the one, pure I and from it emerges the little I, the plurality or "many" of separate existence. When the one becomes identified with the body it becomes many. The concepts of mine and yours arise, of duality. From this false I of many, we have to return to the One.

The one who has understood this world is always happy. If you really understand the true nature of this world, you are freed from the opposites of pleasure and pain. The root of the opposites is the sense of I (egotism) which gives rise to laughter and tears, virtue and sin, and so on. If you let go of the I, recognizing that you are not the doer, you are freed. In the Bhagavad Gita God says, 'You only have the right to act, you have no right to the fruit of your actions. It is I who bestows the fruits of action.'

The Mind Is a Charioteer

How then is a man to return to his source without falling into the pitfalls along his path? The body is like a chariot drawn by the five horses of the sense organs—touch, sight, smell, hearing, and taste (the qualities corresponding to the five elements from which the body is composed). The charioteer is the mind, and in his hands are the reins of the five horses. The passenger being conveyed is the jivatma (individual soul) and as it originates from Paramatma (Universal Soul), its journey is a return. However, the five horses give the charioteer great trouble. The eyes say 'look there' and the skin says 'touch this' and so on. Because of this, there is a constant danger of the horses getting out of control and the chariot meeting with an accident. So the charioteer needs good training as to how to control the horses. He must cultivate discrimination and dispassion.

With the help of his faculties of mind and through the power of his actions, a human being can acquire God-like qualities and uplift humanity by self-sacrifice, as did Jesus, Buddha, and Ram. Or he can acquire demonic qualities like Stalin, Hitler, and Ravanna, and cause suffering and grief to others. Finally, he can earn the title of human being by cultivating friendliness and love toward his fellow man and learn some degree of mind control.

13

Journey of the Soul

"The Rain of God's grace falls and liberates us."

In the Guru Gita, Parvati asks Shiva how the individual Soul returns to God, its source. How to explain such a subtle spiritual subject?

In Mangalore during the monsoon the villagers put up temporary grass huts, but some water drops always leak through the grass roof. As those drops form into puddles on the mud floor, little bubbles or air are forced up to form bubbles on the puddle, where they float and bump together and sometimes merge into a bigger bubble. But in due course they all merge back into the air. Our lives are like that. We are trapped like the air in earth consciousness. The rain of God's grace falls and liberates us from the earth, to merge into the All. Otherwise, there is no particular significance to our lives; just bubbles coming and going, meeting and departing.

Man's situation is therefore similar to a boat going down a broad river to meet the ocean of Paramatma, from where he originates and to whom he is returning. On the left bank are squalid buildings, thorn bushes, and a foul smell; misery, degradation and deprivation reign supreme. The right bank however, has a marble ghat, beautiful buildings, soft green grass, fruit-laden trees and fragrant breezes. The left bank represents hell—sin, pain, disease and death and the right bank represents heaven—pleasure, happiness, and plenty.

By performing good, virtuous actions, a man finds himself on the right bank and by performing egotistical and evil actions, on the left. Actually of the two, the left is preferable because when a man finds himself there he tries his utmost to free himself by performing good actions (punya). The force of his punya propels him to the opposite bank where he soon forgets his previous misery and starts to lose himself in the pleasure of his life there. Soon he forgets that the reason for his existence is to know God and that his goal is to merge into the ocean. After his merit or punya is exhausted, he again finds himself on the left bank of hell.

What then is the solution to the pairs of opposites—pleasure and pain, heaven and hell? A wise man understands his predicament and realizing his destination is the ocean, dedicates all his actions to God. Keeping a watchful eye on both banks, he avoids getting too close to either and steers his boat straight down the middle of the river until he reaches the ocean of God.

> *Babaji is, therefore, very clear that the individual soul's journey is to return to its source. This is called moksha, or self-realization, and there is no real peace until we discover Him in us and us in Him.*
>
> *If the goal of human life is to return to one's spiritual source, how can this be achieved? What is this process by which the individual soul at last merges into the ocean from which it came?*
>
> *The journey can take many forms and in the Indian tradition the four classic yogas are jnan (knowledge), bhakti (devotion), raja (meditation), and hatha (postures). In practice, a seeker (sadhak) will tend to find the correct balance of practices according to his individual temperament and the instructions of his guru. The grace of God and guru and self-effort are often said to be the two wings of the bird of liberation.*

The journey a seeker undertakes is called sadhana. The trials, tribulations, and tests along the way are often known as tapasya. The process of sadhana demands sustained faith and effort, as well as grace. The story of Yudhisthira and his dog is a classic story of the soul's journey and the ways in which it is tested.

Yudhisthira's Journey

After Krishna's death, knowing that it was time for them to die, Draupadi and the five Pandavas went on their last pilgrimage to the place in the Himalayas where earth meets heaven. Only Yudhisthira was virtuous enough to reach the final destination. The others all died at different stages along the way. So, at last Yudhisthira, accompanied by his faithful dog, was met by a heavenly chariot to take him bodily to heaven. However, when his dog was refused entry, Yudhisthira also refused to board the chariot. They had been faithful companions since the beginning of the journey and either they would both be given entry to heaven or neither! At that point, the dog revealed his true form as none other than Yama, the King of Death, whose test Yudhisthira had now passed, thus conquering death himself.

However, his trials were not yet over. Yudhisthira found that nowhere in heaven were his beloved brothers and companions. On asking their whereabouts he was shown a misty region like hell itself, where they had been imprisoned. He resolved, 'I'll stay there with them. Where my loved ones are is my heaven.'

Upon these words the blackness and horror of hell vanished and he passed beyond the appearance of heaven and hell into the true eternal being of God.

In a sense, all the obstacles Yudhisthira encounters on his journey are aspects of his own mind and the misty region represents its confusion and ability to project phantasmagorical images onto reality. Yudhisthira's journey can be seen as an analogy of the Soul's journey to reality and the obstacles it must overcome.

Here, the great mystery of the soul's struggle for emancipation and freedom is analogized. With God-like power and subtlety, the soul projects or creates situations, tests, and scenarios upon the screen of existence, which it then passes through and emerges purified. The Sadhak or seeker is one who understands the various scenarios of life to be opportunities for spiritual growth and ultimate freedom from the dream of phenomenal existence.

Worldly Awareness

Whatever role destiny has given us to perform, we will have to play out to the end. It is true that a man is born with a destiny and that he will have to suffer the fruit of his actions. Some people say there is no reincarnation but it is a fact, nevertheless, that we take birth according to our deeds. Still, even if we cannot escape from our destiny, at least we can do something to lighten its load, its effect on us. If we meditate and contemplate God, we experience bliss and happiness in spite of our past actions. That is the greatness of Sadhana.

However, if your awareness is purely focused on the level of the world of created things and appearances, then you will be besieged by differences: man and woman, beautiful and ugly, young and old. But as your vision becomes more spiritual, everything will start to look the same. All you see, finally, will be God. All countries, castes, young and old are permeated by God, yet God exists independently of all these forms. All is Him, pervading the whole creation.

But we as his creatures love our individual manifestation. Every creature is happy with itself and believes it is great. The skinny, mange-ridden dog whom the children pelt with stones wants to live, not die. The bird that flies says, 'Let me live, I am happy being who I am.' So it is with us.

The Pig and the King's Son

There was once a king who was also a devotee of God. Daily he prayed and practiced spiritual discipline until one day God appeared in his meditation and said, 'All your efforts have born their fruit and after only one more birth, you will come to Me.'

Overjoyed, the King asked the nature of his next and final birth and was aghast to hear that he would take birth as a pig in a certain nearby village.

When he was on his deathbed, he called his eldest son and confided in him the vision he had received. Overruling his son's protests, he made him promise that after waiting a certain time, the son should go to a nearby village and cut the throat of the pig there, thus liberating the soul of the king, his father. With this parting message, the king died.

After the specified time had elapsed, the king's son went to the village to fulfill his promise. After inquiring from a passing villager he found an old dilapidated building and inside it was an enormous sow lying in filth grunting contentedly with a string of piglets squealing and suckling on her teats. Brandishing the knife he had brought for the job, the son advanced toward the sow, who suddenly saw him and said, 'No, don't do it! I am very content here and my life here is very good. Anyway, if you kill me, who will look after my babies?'

•   •   •

Therefore, we have to rise above the awareness of identification with our particular manifestation. We must transcend the world of jivatma (individual soul) and attain the awareness of Paramatma (universal soul). Only then will we be able to see the real situation, the truth.

Kali Yuga

One day a man from Swami Muktananda's ashram in Ganeshpuri asked about the present era, its pitfalls, and how to avoid falling into them. Babaji asked if the man had heard of a

91

scripture called Guru Charitra. *Babaji advised everyone present of the book's greatness and added that it contains many stories and spiritual upadesh (teaching). It also includes the* Guru Gita, *which is a song in which Shiva tells Parvati the secrets of the guru-disciple relationship.*

Babaji added that the book contained a story which answered the man's question.

Brahma, the creator, was holding court one day when suddenly a naked, demonic figure appeared dancing wildly in front of the assembled company. One hand held a long, slobbering tongue and the other, his sex organ. Outraged at this desecration of protocol and decency, Brahma ordered the creature seized, whereupon he shouted, 'In Kali Yuga (the present iron age) I will take over the world by my power. By giving rise to the mis-use and perversion of the sex organ and the tongue, through speaking deceit, slander, and lies, I will degrade and control the entire world. Even great sages and sanyassis will fall by my power.'

The court was appalled to hear this and Brahma made Kali promise not to affect those doing sincere, intense, spiritual sadhana and those singing the name of God. Because of the difficulty in maintaining silence during Kali Yuga, the singing of God's name is especially emphasized though other practices such as satsang and the darshan of saints are also included.

A special paradoxical characteristic is that an earnest devotee can achieve during Kali Yuga, in a very short time, what in other yugas would take very long. Babaji's emphasis here was that a sincere seeker could achieve spiritual knowledge very quickly and that he should not feel downhearted or adversely influenced by the apparent perversity of the age.

Nevertheless, we should not forget the element of effort involved in the sadhana process.

Making butter from milk is hard work and we have to do the work ourselves. Similarly, it is we ourselves who have to churn the milk of the mind in order to separate the butter of atma, which dwells hidden within it. We cannot hope our guru is going to do this work for us!

The Fruits of Tapasya—Swing, Bud and Blossom

Once there was a pundit who used to tell beautiful stories or fables which attracted listeners in many different regions. He would tell his audience, 'If you want to give dakshina, give me money earned through the sweat of your brow. Only this money swings, buds, and blossoms.'

One day he visited a kingdom and as usual told his fables. His listeners grew until they included the king and his ministers. Just before he was to leave, the king thought to himself, 'I do no hard work and have no money earned with the sweat of my brow. But this pundit tells such beautiful stories, I must give him what he asks for.'

So one night he shed his king's apparel and dressed as a poor man. Approaching a blacksmith he asked for work making the steel bands which are then fitted around bullock cart wheels.

'Strike this metal all night until it is a fine band and I will give you one anna,' agreed the blacksmith. So the king started pounding the metal with fine blows. He had a good body and soon the sweat began to pour from him. In the morning he took the one anna earned with such effort and returned to the palace. That afternoon was the last appearance of the pundit and was the time when he would be paid his dakshina by those who had been attending his storytelling. It was usual for people to place dakshina in proportion to the amount given by the king. Everyone expected the king to give a large sum, as he looked so pleased! The dakshina plate was handed to the king and everyone watched carefully and then gasped as the king took the one anna and placed it in the plate. His ministers, of course, had to place proportional amounts and everyone, therefore, gave a tiny donation amounting to only a few annas.

93

The pundit looked down and saw the pitiful sum. He continued his story but inside his heart there was great pain. 'I have been telling stories here for a full month. What will I have to support my family?'

Now there happened to be some merchants from his home town there, who said, 'Panditji, you have been here a full month. You must have earned something to be sent to your wife and children at home.'

'What can I do,' replied the pundit. 'A few annas is all I have earned in my month here. What will my wife say? All right, give it to her but say that I am going to travel for another four or five months telling stories before coming home, in order to earn enough.'

Now the merchants were shrewd businessmen and thought, 'What can we buy here that we could sell later at a good profit? We cannot give his wife merely a few annas.'

They decided on lemons and bought five of them and set off. On their way home they happened to pass through a region where the local king's son was very ill. He was unconscious and the king's doctors advised that the only medicine that would save him was one made from lemons. However, there were none to be had in that region and finally, in desperation, the king announced that 10,000 rupees would be given for a lemon. The merchants produced the five lemons and were given 50,000 rupees in return.

So, the kind merchants arrived home and presented the pundit's wife with 50,000 rupees.

'Your husband sent you this money,' they said. Now the wife thought, 'Let me buy a plot of land and build a two-story house.' She bought nice clothes for the children and took on servants and the family lived happily.

After five months the pundit returned and saw his wife standing on the second floor of a big house in a beautiful sari. 'How did you get to look like that?' he asked, 'and to live in a house like this?'

'This is all ours,' she replied. 'It is all the result of the money you sent with the merchants.'

'The money the merchants brought bought this?' he shouted, furious and humiliated.

Now, the merchants heard what was going on and explained what had happened, adding, 'Don't be angry. She has done nothing wrong.'

Then the pundit realized that it was absolutely true. This was, indeed, the fruit of the dakshina given in the kingdom. This was money earned with sweat that swings, buds, and blossoms.

•   •   •

Babaji added, "Money earned through hard work produces good fruit. By eating food earned through personal effort, a person's knowledge and intellect grows. Without effort and hard work, one receives no happiness, but only sorrow."

Similarly, the process of sadhana requires sincere effort and the process of discovering the truth hidden within us is generally accomplished through the stages of puja (worship), japa (recitation of a mantra or mantras), and finally, meditation.

14

Puja, Japa, and Meditation

"Everything is perceived through the medium of the mind and, like a child, one's mind should be pure and not fickle. If water is pure and colorless, we can see down to its depths."

In every spiritual path, purity of mind and heart are emphasized in order that God may be perceived within the seeker. Puja, japa, and meditation are practices which help to achieve this.

Babaji often mentioned puja as a preliminary step to purifying the mind.

Puja and japa are means to focus the mind. What lies beyond them is meditation. As we ourselves are, so we see God. A buffalo probably thinks that God looks like itself! Two horns, four feet, and a tail. Dogs and goats must think along similar lines! That is why in our Hindu religion God is perceived in all forms. Buffaloes, dogs, cows, boars, fish and even trees. Trees, too, must think, 'There must be one enormous tree with many branches and many leaves. That is our God!'

We humans cannot immediately grasp that which has no qualities—the formless. Actually, God is formless but only by fixing your mind on the form can you gradually arrive at the formless. It is reached by totally absorbing yourself in a form. Take a flower. Some people practice this. Stare at it fixedly and it will eventually disappear. If you really concentrate on a person, the same thing will happen. Actually, a person is formless in essence, but he or she cannot comprehend it. However, if one talks about God with attributes, people have something they can grasp, upon which to pin their faith and devotion. Then they will walk in justice, righteousness, and order. But the statues and symbols themselves have no real life. The worship goes to God, not to them. It is only because our minds cannot grasp the Absolute that we use images.

The truth is that the Divine Mother is within us pervading head to toe, but we cannot perceive Her. That is why we objectify Her, the reality, as a statue or yantra, something we can see with the physical senses. Whatever a person thinks and concentrates on, so he becomes.

The Prostitute and the Holy Man

Once a sadhu (holy man) and a prostitute lived opposite each other on a street. The sadhu wore beautiful ochre clothes, gave fine lectures, and had many disciples. The prostitute, on the other hand, carried on her business and supported her two children, fully aware of the lowliness and shamefulness of her situation. Every day she would watch the sadhu through her window and her whole wish was that she could be more like him. The sadhu, on the other hand, every day made a mental note of how many customers she got and during his meditation he would think of her sinfulness, whereas the prostitute's mind dwelled on the greatness and holiness of the sadhu and how much she longed for those qualities within herself. Finally, they both died, strangely enough on the same day, and the sadhu's body was buried with great honor by his many disciples and admirers. The prostitute, however, was burned unceremoniously and no one gave her a thought. Their souls went to be weighed to find where they would go. Amazingly, the sadhu was sentenced to hell, and the prostitute to heaven.

'Wait, there must be some mistake,' shouted the sadhu. 'I was a Sadhu and spent my whole life performing spiritual practices and did everything according to the scriptures. This slut spent her time entertaining men, selling her body for money.'

The answer came back, 'Yes, because your body observed fasts and rituals it got an honored burial, whereas her body, because she misused it, got an ignominious end. However, because of her repentance and constant contemplation of your apparent virtues and holiness, her mind has attained great purity. Consequently, she goes to heaven. You, however, spent your time obsessed with her sinfulness and great faults in the eyes of God and so your mind has become dense and sinful. For this reason you will have to go to hell.'

In spite of Babaji's recognition of the validity of puja as a practice, he would always point a seeker beyond blind faith in ritual to the living presence in the heart.

Where there is faith there is God. It is our faith which grants us spiritual fruit.

Once a European had brought a small sandalwood statue of Ganesh for Babaji. In feigned exasperation he said,

I don't want any more Gods! If I accept him, I'll have to do puja to him daily and if I don't he will get angry with me. Look, he has such a big belly. How can I keep him fed? Here, you take him! [handing it back to the European]

I am neither Hindu, Christian, nor Muslim. It is the heart that is important. Indeed, it is because we do not know the heart that we externalize the indweller, God, and create a statue to worship. This is merely a stage in order to learn concentration. In the last phase of spiritual evolution we do not use statues. For example, sanyassis do not worship anything external.

> *Babaji's work here as a teacher was always to draw the listener's attention to the real holy place and temple, the spiritual heart residing within us all. Like every spiritual teacher, he would again and again expose the human tendency to create idols out of religion and encouraged us to avoid the kind of foolish blind faith that gives rise to superstition, ignorance, and fundamentalism.*

Akbar and Birbal's Shoe—the True Holy Place

Once Akbar, the great Moghul king, the subject of many amusing stories, and Birbal, his astute minister, were arguing about the value of holy places.

Birbal secretly stole one of the king's shoes, buried it in a certain spot and started doing pradakshina (circumambulating) around it at special times. Some local people noticed and realized that this must be a holy spot so they too, started circumambulating it and even holding prayers there. Soon their faith bore fruit and some of their prayers were answered. Grateful devotees built a small shrine until eventually the place was besieged with pilgrims. At last Akbar himself came to know about this new and famous holy place and he, too, became a pilgrim. Turning to Birbal he inquired as to what was actually there. Perhaps the Samadhi of a great holy man?

'No, your Majesty,' was Birbal's gentle reply, 'the samadhi of your shoe!'

Japa

> *There is no doubt that Babaji was a great advocate of japa, the recitation of a mantra. He stressed that japa was a vital preliminary to meditation, which occurs "beyond" japa often when the mantra repeated by a seeker spontaneously ceases. However, he emphasized*

the importance of receiving a mantra from a qualified guru who had himself perfected it (see chapter 9, Guru and Disciple).

Babaji generally initiated seekers into the mantras he himself had used during his own sadhana, which included the nine-syllabled Devi mantra and the guru mantra. There were also daily recitations of the Guru Gita, Shiva Mahimna, as well as various bhajans and chants. However, he also stressed that puja and japa should be accompanied by a genuine sincerity of purpose if they are to bear fruit. Only then can the effort made be called tapasya and the fruits can be used for the welfare of others. We should not be like the brahmin in the following story.

The Brahmin's Three Wishes

There was once a brahmin. Now, brahmins are often a little poor, so to fill his stomach he would do a little astrology for people, in exchange for food. Now, with the passing of time, the brahmin's wife grew old, her teeth all fell out and she grew hunched and gray. On his visits to other houses to make astrological predictions for his clients, he would notice that they often had beautiful wives, unlike his own.

Finally, he decided to do tapasya, recite certain mantras, so that his wife would also become beautiful. He decided to go to a solitary mountain like our Sapta Shringh and perform austerities. But first he told his wife to make some laddoos (sweets) as big as tennis balls! Armed with these, he went to the mountain where there was a cave with a good supply of water and did his penance, in between mouthfuls of laddoo and gulps of water!

This went on for some days until it happened that Shiva and Parvati were traveling overhead in an airplane on their way from Kashi to Bombay!

'Who is that down there?' asked Parvati.

'Oh, just a brahmin eating laddoos and saying a mantra,' replied Shankar cautiously.

101

'Come on,' said Parvati, 'let's bestow a boon on him.'

Because of her insistence, they descended and approached the brahmin. Reluctantly, Shiva picked up three stones and gave them to the brahmin. 'With these,' he promised, 'you can make any wish you like.'

Overjoyed, the brahmin returned home. The first person he saw was his wife. Gums gaping, face all screwed up, she hobbled toward him. The brahmin took a pebble and waved it above her head.

'Oh, God, make my wife into the most beautiful woman in the world.' Immediately her hair became black, her teeth reappeared, and she stood up straight and beautiful.

'What shall I do now?' wondered the brahmin. 'My wife is so beautiful that if anyone sees her they will abduct her. What shall I do with her?'

'Stay indoors,' he finally told her. 'Don't let anyone see you. A valuable possession must be well-protected.' He gave her some pots.

'Here, you can use these for your ablutions but do not go outside. I'll empty them later.'

So she just stayed indoors eating and lazing until one day a local ruffian saw her through the window. 'Oh ho, so our brahmin's keeping a mistress, is he?' he thought. Breaking open the door, he forcibly abducted her and carried her off to his own dwelling.

When the brahmin found out what had happened he was furious. Grasping his remaining stones, he set out for the ruffian's house. When he found it he started shouting abuses and threats, much to the ruffian's amusement.

'If you don't clear off, I'll come and finish you off,' threatened the ruffian.

'Finish me off, will you,' thought the enraged brahmin. He took the second stone and wished.

'Oh, God, make my wife into a tiger so that she finishes off this rascal.'

Immediately his wife became a tiger. Catching hold of her

abductor she struck him dead and joined her husband. When they got home, the brahmin took a look at her. 'Now what can I do? I'm a man and she's a tiger!' he moaned.

Taking out the third stone, he wished, 'God, make my wife as she was before. Make her an old woman again.'

• • •

Babaji smiled. The meaning of this story is that those who do not perform real sadhana receive no real fruit. The brahmin had performed 'laddoo sadhana' and this was the result.

However, when a person bows to the Divine Mother in sincerity and humility, She will immediately grant the desires of that person's heart. Furthermore, if a noble person asks the Mother for the well-being of others, She is eager and pleased to bless them.

Meditation

Japa is greater than puja but dhyana (meditation) is the highest worship and grants knowledge. Knowledge, like love, gives rise to more knowledge. Just as we need a little capital to earn money, similarly we use our knowledge to accumulate more. Meditation is the best means to achieve steadiness. In my opinion it also implies contemplation. Where have I come from? Where am I going? What is this world?

Certainly by using a mantra given by a qualified guru, with correct understanding, a person can achieve peace. "Om Namah Shivayah" (I bow to the Supreme Principle) is not, in fact, a Hindu mantra but universal. "Om Guru" is important. The scriptures say that without guru there can be no knowledge. Guru is not a particular body or person. Mantra itself is guru and has been handed down to us by the ancient sages. Contemplating mantra (japa) leads to meditation.

If we meditate and contemplate God, what happens is that our awareness stays with God and we feel blissful and happy in spite of our particular destiny and karma. That is the greatness of meditation. Even if we cannot avoid our individual karma, at least we can rise above its adverse effects.

What is meditation? Meditation is focusing the mind, making it one-pointed. If you direct your mind to something you learn from it without anyone teaching you [Babaji picks up the large magnifying glass lying beside him]. Take this magnifying glass. Just by looking at it with the full power of the mind you can learn something about it. What does it do? How is it made? What is the principle behind it?

The human birth is the highest. Why? Humans have the capacity for jnana and vijnana. With this power, human beings can visit the moon and other planets. If you want to cultivate jnan and vijnan, you can do it by meditation.

How does one meditate? Meditation is within us, it is not something to be acquired from outside. Just sit resolved and tranquil. Do not worry about anything. Then the willpower grows and the power of knowledge grows. You can do japa until, of its own accord, the repetition stops. What lies beyond japa is meditation.

A meditator should master one asana (posture) for meditation. Truly speaking, if you can sit in one position such as padmasana (lotus position) for three hours, you have mastered it. How can you call it meditation to sit for a few minutes and then start shifting your position because of pain. In true meditation a meditator is not aware if pain is there or not. His mind is merged in God, not in the body.

> *Once an American complained to Babaji of fear. Babaji took him aside and showed him a light in the space between the eyebrows.*

That light is your own atma. It is not something I have given you. Practice looking at that space and within a few days you will see it effortlessly and your fears will disappear. There are nine different lights perceived in meditation. Sometimes you will see an expanse of blue surrounding something. That "something" is the truth and compared to that the various experiences have little value.

The Blue Bindu

The blue bindu can be seen with eyes open or closed. Just sit and concentrate and a tiny point the size of a tapioca seed will appear. Actually, our bodies are full of them and without them you would not be alive. It comes and goes but finally comes to rest in our vision. My Maharaj (guru) used to say that anyone who has a devotional leaning always has the bindu accompanying him. Actually it is the light of the bindu (manifested light of the supreme soul) that accompanies us throughout our life. But one should go beyond that light and merge in the formless. More than seeing God, become It! Many people see the bindu but their bad actions continue as before. Have they been freed from anything? No. But after merging in God all past sins are destroyed.

You see, the blue bindu is the form emanating from the Absolute. Rays arise from the sun and can be seen. If you reach the sun itself then neither you nor the rays remain. When an individual ray merges with the sun will it be any different from the sun itself? Do you understand? Look at my hand, for example. Here is the sun [Babaji points to his palm] from which "rays" shoot out in all directions. If a ray should return back into the sun, will it still be an individual ray? No! Similarly, the blue bindu will be with you until you merge with the Absolute.

Nada

Sometimes in a quiet place you will hear a sound called nada. Once your mind gets accustomed to listening to it and to perceiving that light, your fears will vanish. There are nine kinds of nada, such as the sounds of: crickets; water thrown onto a hot plate; distant rain; cymbals; a faraway bell; and a flute.

One who regularly hears nada does not take future births. In the early hours of the morning between 3:00 a.m. and 6:00 a.m. we can sit and contemplate it and the light, and then come to understand that which dwells within us. Nada is the sound of consciousness. When you begin to listen, your mind gets absorbed in it. The mind's exhaustion departs and it becomes fresh again. If you then contemplate a problem your mind will quickly arrive at a decision.

Everything that can be seen, including visions, is, however, still within the realm of the mind and implies duality—subject and object. The true state is when we merge with the object of meditation. We meditate in order to attain No—thing (shunya). Compared to that, the different experiences of meditation have little value. That No—thing is our true home. Some people think that Siddhaloka (a heavenly abode for perfected beings) or some other place (loka) is the goal. Actually, these are just more places. One day everyone has to return to where they have come from. We have come from the ocean of God and return there.

Truth and perfection are one. You cannot perceive them because they are beyond perception. You can, however, become them. From sea comes salt but when salt is immersed in the sea it becomes the sea. Similarly, if a drop enters the ocean, it becomes the ocean. If a drop is removed from the ocean, is not the ocean potential in the drop?

15

Discrimination

"Our lack of discrimination causes so much trouble."

One of Swamiji's favorite subjects was discrimination between the real and the unreal. In fact, the peeling away of ignorance in order to allow the light of truth to shine through may be said to be the essence of all spiritual paths.

The fact is that it is the mind which stands between us and God and when mind becomes steady, we perceive Him.

Devotion to a master and practices such as meditation, chanting, and puja are all instrumental in sharpening the faculty of discrimination. In addition, absolute vigilance is required to combat the mind's tendency toward dullness and inertia, which cloud the intellect and obstruct the light of the spirit.

To illustrate this need for discrimination in spiritual life, Babaji told a story.

The Disciple and the Elephant

Once there was a guru who used to tell his disciples 'all is God.' One disciple felt he had truly imbibed this teaching and one day went outside to find people running, panic-stricken. Suddenly a warning shout came, 'Rogue elephant.'

However, the disciple thought to himself, 'Why should I run away? After all, if everything is God, then so is the elephant and it won't harm me!'

Just then the *mahut* came running down the road shouting, 'Get off the road! Rogue elephant!'

The disciple, however, stood his ground in the middle of the road and was almost hurled to the ground by the elephant. Suddenly his guru was standing in front of him. 'Why didn't you move off the road?' he asked.

'Guruji,' replied the disciple, 'it was you who told me all was God. You told a lie.'

'You fool,' replied Guruji, 'wasn't that mahut who told you to move aside also God? Why didn't you listen to *that* God?'

> *Even the great jnanis are themselves not immune to their discrimination being clouded, especially by the evil of bad company.*

At the end of the Mahabharata war, the great jnani and warrior Bhishma was lying on his bed of arrows expounding on dharma while surrounded by the Pandavas, Krishna, Draupadi, and others.

Suddenly Draupadi could bear no more and cried, 'Where was all your dharma and fine philosophy when I was being stripped publicly in Duryodhana's court and you just looked on and did nothing? One word from you and I would have been set free!'[3]

[3]This refers to a famous scene in the epic, Mahabharata, of Draupadi's public humiliation by Duryodhana. She prayed to the Lord, who responded with the miracle of Draupadi's sari, which was being stripped off her body, becoming endlessly long. Her honor was thus saved.

Bhishma, the great jnani, sadly agreed. 'See the evil result of accepting the food, company, and hospitality of a corrupt man (Duryodhana) and how clouded my intellect became as a result.'

In practice, truth and untruth invariably exist side by side.

There will always be light and dark, fire and smoke, good and bad. What is important is to contemplate the bright flame, not the smoke.

The glory of the master is that he is instrumental in removing the veil of ignorance and duality. Once Baba Muktananda had asked one of his students to show him her earrings, which happened to be artificial. Disappearing indoors, he emerged with another pair which he presented to her, saying, 'Take these, they are real. That is my job, to replace the unreal with the real.'

The tendency on every level of human life, however, is to revere illusion and appearances and we often pay a heavy price for our foolishness and lack of discrimination. This tendency was the subject of many of Swamiji's stories and often his warnings about the gullibility of human nature inevitably extended into the delicate domain of religion.

A story that Swamiji often told with a certain humorous relish was the true story of the Narayan Darshan cult which once existed in India.

A certain Sadhu made money from a gullible public by giving darshan in a dark room dressed as Narayan (Vishnu). Behind him would stand a disciple holding conch and discus and together they gave an impression of the four-armed Vishnu. A person was granted darshan for a split second and then shown out of the room. Strangely enough, much money was collected in this way.

A grisly extension to this story, which Babaji often related, is that a disciple of the above false prophet was a thief and had his nose cut off as a punishment. As a kind of revenge on society, he succeeded in starting a cult called nag sampraya (nose dynasty) where he gave initiation in which he surgically removed the initiate's nose. The initiate's blind belief was that he or she would then be able to see God. It seems that the cult had a good number of members, all of whom swore that they could now perceive God. Eventually, the wise old minister of a gullible king, who was considering joining the cult, managed to expose the fraud and place all the members under arrest. Whereupon, they confessed that they had been hypnotized and had never had any vision of God whatsoever.

Swamiji was always quick to point out that a king or important man of the world is often vulnerable to the foolishness of the world and is often in sore need of guidance. Indeed, if we use our discrimination, it becomes apparent that the rich and famous, contrary to appearances, are often to be pitied rather than emulated.

Wealth and the Rich

People think that to be a big or important person is very good, very wonderful. However, in practice what happens? In the case of Indira Ghandhi, wherever she goes police accompany her and doctors check her food in case it is poisoned.[4]

She is not even free to walk down the street by herself or she will be mobbed. She cannot speak freely because all her words are written in newspapers and taped. One word too many and she gets criticized. Every moment her mind is occupied with running the country so she never gets a moment's peace. Even her toilet has to be checked by security guards. If she goes anywhere, they surround her front and back. Tell me, isn't that how a convict is treated? A convicted murderer? Even my guru had so many people around him he never had a moment's peace. A poor man, however, can eat anywhere, go anywhere, do anything he wishes freely, and gets good sleep at night!

---

[4]Ironically, she was later assassinated by her own security guards.

110

All things were created by God for Himself. He gives us wisdom and works through us Himself. One person is poor, another rich. It is His play, His leela. For Him, the poor person is the same as the wealthy one. The same sunshine falls on both. But if it is very cold, the poor person has the strength to endure it. The rich man requires an overcoat. God gives the poor strength to endure hardship. This is one of His rules.

The rich never enjoy any real peace. They consider themselves very intelligent and think they have gathered their wealth by means of their superior intellect. The truth is, often they take the share of others for themselves. What they really gather is sin. If a man wants to make a pile of earth, he has to dig a hole to get it. However, he doesn't see the hole he has made but only his little pile. If only he had allowed himself to see that gaping hole he would realize his mistake. Of course, a man needs some money to live on but he should not amass more than he needs. Generally, the more money you have, the more problems. To make money is not too difficult. To use it well is not so easy.

Vishnu and Laxmi

One day, Vishnu, a barber by profession, who often cut Babaji's hair, arrived. Vishnu, with his amiable grin of buck teeth stained with red betel nut, was an irresistible and ready source of humor, especially as he shared his name with Vishnu, the Preserver of the Hindu Trinity.

Babaji's habit was always to joke with him and with a mischievous smile he asked Vishnu, 'How is everything in Vaikuntha (Vishnu's heaven)?'

'Well, Maharaj' was the reply, 'samsara [life in this world] just keeps going.' Everyone in the room roared with laughter, where-upon Babaji told a story.

111

'Once Lord Vishnu was lying recumbent on Shesh, the primal serpent in the ocean of milk, with Laxmi (Vishnu's consort) massaging his legs. He was obviously in a pensive mood, so when Narada the wandering minstrel arrived to see the Lord, he remarked, 'Lord, why are you looking so worried?'

'Laxmi is my problem' came the reply, and seeing Narada's bewilderment, he added, 'Look, and I'll demonstrate why.'

So Lord Vishnu, the sustainer of the three worlds, took the form of a pundit in a little town where he started giving daily spiritual discourses of such charm, power, beauty, and wisdom, that soon the entire village population locked up house and went to listen. Men, women, and children sat spellbound and soon devotion for God, joy, and harmony transformed the little town into a veritable heaven.

Of course, where Vishnu is, Laxmi is bound to follow, so, sure enough, in the form of an old crone, Vishnu's consort also arrived in the town. Just as the daily discourse was about to begin, she went to an old lady asking for water. Hurriedly, so as not to miss the start of the day's discourse, she handed over the lota (metal container) of water, which, upon touching Laxmi's hand, turned to gold.

'Hey, this isn't my lota, it's solid gold,' gasped the old lady.

'Yes, I'm afraid that my hand has this quality that everything it touches tends to become gold. Keep it,' replied the crone.

By the next day, the news had spread and, instead of attending the Lord's discourse, several ladies were waiting at home hoping for a visit from Laxmi! They were not disappointed and soon the townsfolk were acquiring gold pots, plates and the like. Soon not one person was there for the pundit's discourse as the menfolk also got diverted by the promise of this new source of wealth.

Now, Lord Vishnu, who is the prisoner only of true devotion, with no one to hold Him there, left that town and, of course, where Vishnu goes, Laxmi follows. So she also left and soon the town declined to its old ways. Devotion to God grew dim and the new-found prosperity waned and again the people returned to their old life.

•   •   •

Babaji remarked with a meaningful glance at the visitors in the room, "So, hold on to devotion to God (Vishnu) and certainly Laxmi won't be far away with her blessings and gifts. But don't go running after Laxmi and forget Vishnu, otherwise He'll leave and she will follow!"

How, then, to keep our minds and hearts bright and clean enough to withstand and renounce the tendency of the mind toward the glitter of illusion?

16

Renunciation

"It is not necessary to cut yourself off from the world in order to realize God."

For Babaji, renunciation had little to do with wearing particular clothes, having a long beard, or even becoming a sanyassi. It meant to renounce the small 'I'—the ahamkara (ego).

Jiva means individual soul. Soul is born from Brahman, in essence is one with Brahman. But the soul remains small (undeveloped) because of the little self or ego which conceals the Universal Self. The little self must go.

Some people say the body is destroyed at death, but not so, the bodily elements merge with their constituent components and continue to live as other life forms growing from the soil, such as rice or wheat. Nor does the soul die, as it comes from Brahman, which is eternal and one day returns to Brahman. So what is perishable, what experiences fluctuations? What is the relationship between Jiva and *Atman*? What is the source, and also ultimate end of the little self which keeps Jiva, soul, apart from Atman or Brahman? The qualities of the little self (ego) are sometimes called the six enemies—pride, lust, greed, envy, anger, and delusion. These are the personal possessions or pets of Jiva. If the soul did not feed these pets they would not be there. The analogy is a pet dog; you play with it, feed it, enjoy the dog's company. But if you had knowledge that the dog is not beneficial, you would renounce it and force it to leave. But you like the dog, keep it near you, fondle it, enjoy its company. So the dog stays with you. Very few people have the maturity of under-standing to tell the dog—the six enemies—to leave them. Only then will the soul experience Brahman, the eternal state of awareness beyond happiness and grief.

Anger

Ideally, one should be free from anger, but, in practice, as long as one eats, one has the capacity for anger! When it arises, do not keep it in your stomach. Let it emerge, but without causing harm to others. Don't hold anger inside you, otherwise it will burn you up. Anger is a fire which burns if suppressed. The eyes become red, the body shakes, the heart quickens. You rapidly become like a fool. Your anger climbs up to the brain and wisdom vanishes. Anger always arises from ignorance, never from wisdom. Even if you have been very angry, this state does not last long. You soon become peaceful again, but your radiance has dimmed. Anger consumes your vital power, your wisdom. That is why it is not worth being angry. A wise man does not get angry with another. Laughing inside, he goes on his way, thinking, 'Who am I to teach this person a lesson? God is the real teacher.'

If you must be angry, let it be directed at another's bad qualities, not at them. Of course, sometimes anger is also necessary for self-preservation. If you never show it, others will dominate you. Haven't you heard the story about the snake?

A certain snake used to terrorize the villagers who passed along the path where it lived, until a holy man influenced it to become meek and kindly! Some time later, the holy man passed by and met the snake, which was now bedraggled and weak. Surprised, he asked the snake what the matter was and received the answer that now he was no longer a threat, the village boys took advantage and threw stones at him.

'Brother snake,' said the holy man, 'I told you not to terrorize the villagers. I didn't tell you not to hiss when they tried to take advantage of you.

Renunciation and Worldly Life

A young Australian arrived who had practiced meditation for some considerable time and was now visiting different teachers.

You don't have to run here and there looking for teachers and getting involved in their organizations. The Sadguru is within and you should seek and find him there. The path already shown to you is good and you can use the mantra given you.

Babaji told a story to illustrate that we have already been given everything we need if only we can perceive and accept it.

The Adivasi Girl

Once there was a simple *Adivasi* girl who decided she should marry as high up as possible and not one of her own caste. To find the highest was now her all-consuming object. Observing a likely looking businessman, she followed him to the collector's office (top local government official) where he paid his respects to the collector. Realizing that the collector was obviously higher than the business-man, immediately the girl decided to set her sights on him instead. Now, it so happened that the same day the collector happened to be visiting the king, whom he obsequiously greeted as one higher than himself. Following the king, she observed him call on a famous brahmin and give him dakshina and apply *kum kum* to his forehead.

'Surely this brahmin must be the highest,' she thought. But the following morning the brahmin went to pay his respects to a Sadhu, who in his turn went and prostrated in front of a stone Shiva lingam. The girl sadly concluded that the stone lingam was the highest of all, when a dog came and urinated on it. Amazed, she was staring at the dog when suddenly the dog's owner, a young Adivasi man, whistled and the dog went and obediently licked his feet.

Seeing this, she cried with joy and relief at the justice and goodness of God's ways and married the Adivasi. Having gone full circle, she had found her way back to herself.

•　　•　　•

Babaji looked at the young Austrailan lovingly.

When you return to your country, do some service and do not run away from your responsibility to the world. It is the world which has given you birth and you should do something in return. For example, if you have a business, you might be able to give employment to ten people and support their families. This is real service to God. Just to fill your own stomach isn't difficult. Go out into the world, earn well, and do good. There is nothing wrong with earning well and we can do good for others. What we need we can use and the rest we can put to good use.

Action

You cannot escape performing actions. Whether you sleep, walk, eat, think, or write, all are actions. However, if you do something, do it well! Don't worry about whether it will be of use to you. All the souls in this world are the same as yours, so even if a human being doesn't benefit from your actions, then perhaps an animal or bird will.

Even if you try to do nothing, the inner controller will cause you to act, saying 'Now, go.' or 'Do this.' This is why it is said— 'salutations to the Goddess who dwells in all beings in the form of the intellect.'

It is not necessary to cut yourself off from the world in order to realize God. It is God who has become the world and to cut yourself off from it is an insult to Him. It is attachment (moha) which has to be cut off. Many saints have been married, so don't reject worldly life.

The Two Friends

Do you know about the two friends who set out together to find God?

For a while they moved place to place living on alms. Finally, they reached a small village and one of them said, 'I'm going to stay here. I'm tired of this life of roaming and begging.' So he did and in due course married a local girl, had several children, built a house, and had a flourishing business.

His friend, on the other hand, continued on his pilgrimage visiting many holy spots, performed many austerities and rituals, and some years later found himself in the same village as he had left his friend all those years ago. Upon making inquiries he was shown to a house, and knocking on the door, was greeted by his old friend. Embracing each other tearfully, they sat down to a welcoming meal cooked by his wife. The householder lovingly questioned his mendicant friend, who admitted, 'After all these years of searching for God, I really cannot say I have found Him. And how about you?'

'Well, yes, I can say that I found not only Bhagwan (the "male" aspect of God) but also Bhagwati (the "female" Divine energy)!'

'Can you show me, too?' cried the mendicant.

'Of course,' replied his friend and called out, 'Ram! Krishna! Ganga! Saraswati!'

Immediately his wife, sons, and daughters came in from outside and he introduced them to his friend.

'You see, Bhagwan has taken the form of my wife and children. I served Bhagwan and now He serves me. If I am tired and aching, Bhagwan massages me and if I am hungry, cooks for me. In my old age I want for nothing and am happy.'

The Sanyassi

Sanyas is in the mind, not in the color of the cloth a man wears or whether his head is shaven.

> *Although Swamiji was a Sanyassi for more than twenty-five years, he seldom encouraged his disciples to seek the robe of Sanyassa. In spite of that, he was highly regarded by sanyassis and sadhus who often came for his darshan. One day a Spanish Sanyassi arrived to see Babaji. His guru had died and he wanted to move on from the big ashram and organization which had given him sanyas. At the same time, he felt deeply indebted to it, which made it difficult for him to make the break. Babaji told him:*

A sanyassi is a dead man. All his worldly obligations are served. He is free. In the old days a Sanyassi would not stay in one place but would keep moving, living off alms. Now, times have changed. I am not saying you should not stay and work for the ashram, nor am I saying to leave it. The important thing is not to feel attached. If you feel you have to stay in one place, then it becomes a jail. Does a man take sanyas to go to jail?

Shiva lives in a graveyard but gives everything to others.[5]

---

[5]Shiva is often depicted as a renunciant or ascetic. A beautiful house was once built for him and all the Gods hoped he would live in it. However, Shiva presented it to Vishnu, saying it was fit for him as protector of the world.

He is content to live in a graveyard. A great man is one who makes or creates something and then gives it away to another.

> *Significantly, Babaji did just this when in 1980, he handed over the Sapta Shringh Ashram he had founded with such hardship to Swami Omananda, his disciple. On occasions people would ask him why he seldom visited Sapta Shringh for more than a few hours after 1980.*

Once a father has given away his daughter, does he then ask for her back?

•   •   •

The important thing is to take sanyas within oneself. Sanyas isn't given or taken, one becomes it. It is not a question of cloth! If a sanyassi comes to realize that he doesn't have the qualities of a sanyassi, then it may be better for him to avoid hypocrisy and shed the cloth.

The Sadhu and the Loincloth

Have you heard the story of the sadhu and the loincloth?

Once a Sadhu lived by himself in a little hut in the forest. He had almost no possessions, only one spare loincloth to his name, which he used to wash and hang up to dry. One day a family of mice arrive and took a liking to his spare loincloth! Finding it full of holes the next morning, he complained to a wealthy visiting disciple, who suggested that a cat should be kept in order to control the mice. So the Sadhu decided to keep a cat.

'But what about milk to feed the cat?' he asked the disciple.

'Well, Maharaj, for that you will need a cow,' came the answer. So a cow was also provided and the cat had milk to drink.

121

'But who will look after the cow?' demanded the Sadhu.

'Oh, you will need a man for that, Maharaj,' came the reply. So a man was appointed to look after the cow and stayed in a nearby hut.

This arrangement worked well, except that the cowherd would often be absent, explaining, 'Maharaj, I have to go to my wife and children.'

Finally, the Sadhu suggested, 'Why don't you bring your family here?' So the family came and lived in the cowherd's hut. After some days of observation, the Sadhu thought to himself, 'What a good life these people have! They seem happy and joyful whereas I am usually bad-tempered and sullen. Perhaps I should get married, too!'

So he did! From one loincloth to a full-fledged worldly life!

Babaji often talked of the characteristics of true sanyas and its opposite, cat sanyas, which he explained as follows.

Cat Sanyas

Once there lived a cat who was a relentless hunter of rats. All the rats in the house lived in mortal terror of him until one day one of the rats noticed him lying in a strange, immobile position. After some time, when the cat still did not move, the rat approached closer but there was no sign of life. Finally, the rat called his brothers and sisters and they all gathered in awed silence around their old enemy. Had he perhaps died? Finally, one daring rat reached out and touched him. Slowly the cat looked up and with a look of meek repentance, said, 'Oh, rats, how sinful I am. I have been killing and eating your family members for all this time. Such bad karma I have earned for myself through such sinful acts. I am thinking that the only possible atonement is to go to Kashi and end my life in the Ganges, which they say washes away all sins.'

On seeing this astonishing change of heart, the chief rat said, 'Oh, cat, please take us also so that we, too, can see holy Kashi and get moksha.'

The cat agreed and they all set off in a long line with the cat at the rear. One by one the cat killed and ate the last in line until at last the chief rat looked around and noticed the missing family members.

'Oh, cat,' he asked, 'where are the rest of my brothers and sisters?' One look at the cat and he realized what had happened and escaped.

•   •   •

This is called cat sanyas and Babaji urged us to beware of the false prophets and teachings which abound. The public is in many respects gullible and foolish and a person must be careful when he chooses a spiritual path or a guru, for the spiritual path is full of charlatans, frauds, and assorted pitfalls.

It is sometimes good to keep a certain distance from things. If you see a mountain from a distance it looks beautiful. However, if you actually climb it you may find ravines, thorns, snakes, heat, and cold. Every difficulty of the place you will directly experience. So it is good to keep a distance from what may harm us.

A true sadhu should help others as much as he can. This is all the Lord's play. One should not see distinctions but rather see all with the eye of equality. This is the sanyassi's dharma. All religions must be seen to be as true as the other and their members as forms of the Lord Himself.

17

The Jnani

*"His word and blessing has so much power
that it supersedes even the law of karma."*

The jnani, it is said, is a mirror or transparency for the Supreme
Self. For those fortunate enough to come into contact with him,
mystical ideals such as truth, knowledge, God, love, and joy can
become a reality, an actual experience. The mirror the jnani holds
in front of the aspirant is none other than himself and the reflection
seen is the aspirant's own true nature. For the individual soul and
Universal Consciousness, say the scriptures, are one in essence.

Babaji's work was primarily then to serve as this mirror for the
Supreme Self. On occasions he would also actively intercede on
behalf of those who approached him. Babaji's power to intercede on
behalf of others and grant blessings can be attested to by literally
hundreds of people and it would be impossible as well as unnecessary
to record more than a very few of them. This power had been won
by his years of penance at Sapta Shringh and elsewhere and his
devotion to the Divine Mother. Babaji delighted in telling the story
of Narad and the agaram bagaram Baba, to illustrate God's love
for his saints and the power of their word. There are quite a number

*of hilarious and probably deliberate similarities between the agaram
bagaram Baba in the story and himself. Indeed, Babaji's favorite
description for himself was 'agaram bagaram!'*

Lord Vishnu and the Agaram Bagaram Baba

Once Narada, the wandering minstrel and friend of Lord Vishnu,
was on his way through a small village when a woman recognized
him and came running up. In tears, she begged for the boon of a
child, as she and her husband had no issue. Touched to the heart,
Narada promised to ask Lord Vishnu personally about the matter. On
being told of the woman's request, the Lord retorted that this
particular woman wasn't destined to give birth in her next three
incarnations, which Narad sadly conveyed to the unfortunate
couple.

Now it so happened that near this same village was a mountain.
There, in a cave lived an agaram bagaram Baba who spent his whole
life in devotion to God and only rarely emerged from his cave. One
day, however, he made his way to the village and started shouting out
'one chappati, one child; two chappatis, two children, three chappatis,
three children!' On hearing this the barren woman grabbed three
chappatis and ran to the agaram bagaram Baba and lovingly and
hopefully placed them in his hand. In due course she gave birth to
three children.

Some time after the birth of her third child, Narada again
happened to be passing by. Stopping off to greet the woman of
unfortunate destiny, he was astonished to see her and her husband
surrounded by three children.

'Whose are these, mother?' he asked.

'Ours,' she smiled.

'Impossible. The Lord Himself told me so,' replied Narada. So
the couple explained about the agaram bagaram Baba living on the
mountain and his blessing. Furious and humiliated, Narada imme-

diately set off for *Vaikuntha* to voice his displeasure at the unreliability of the Lord's word, to Vishnu Himself.

On arrival, he noticed people running here and there and on coming into the Lord's presence was horrified to see him lying in pain groaning.

'The only medicine that can alleviate the Lord's pain is made from the liver of a true devotee,' explained the doctor. 'Narada, can you get one?'

Immediately Narada set off and started asking people if they would donate their liver for the Lord who was ill. Although in theory many were willing, in practice everyone had a reason for not being able to donate their liver. One was about to marry, another had to look after his aging parents and so on. Finally, Narada found himself in the same village and spotted the woman and her husband. He hastily explained the urgent crisis in Vaikuntha, whereupon the husband interrupted, 'Well, of course, in ordinary circumstances I would certainly give my liver but now that I have three children to support it is not right for me to sacrifice my body for God. But why not ask the agaram bagaram Baba who lives up on the mountain nearby?'

Even as he said those words, who should come running around the corner but the Baba himself!

'What is this about the Lord being ill and wanting a liver?' he cried. 'Look, here is my whole body for him, not just my liver. Let's go! Take me to the Lord.' So they both set off to Vankuntha where, strange to say, Lord Vishnu was sitting quite normally as if nothing had happened.

'Lord, here is someone willing to give his whole body to you,' exclaimed Narada.

'Not necessary, Narada,' said God, 'I'm fine now. But tell me why you found it necessary to chase all over the three worlds for a liver. Haven't you yourself got a liver? You are supposed to be such a great devotee. Now to answer the question you wished to ask about how a woman destined to bear no children can produce three, you now have the answer practically demonstrated.'

Pointing to the agaram bagaram Baba, the Lord continued, 'Look at this great and true devotee of mine. Because he has given his whole self to Me, and is even willing to give his body without a second thought, his word and blessing has so much power that it supersedes even the law of destiny and karma established by Me.'

•   •   •

The mind of a jnani is always alert to the events around him, no matter how apparently insignificant. Knowing that 'not a leaf moves except by the grace of God,' he also knows that the inscrutable purpose of God is constantly revealing itself for those with eyes to see.

Many extraordinary and even miraculous incidents occur around great mahatmas or jnanis. However, Babaji regarded showy miracles or "feats" with a mixture of distaste and amusement. On one occasion a lady from Bombay supposedly possessed of the ability to perform such "feats" arrived at Babaji's Nasik bungalow. Dramatically, she entered the room with several of her admirers and suddenly perfumed ash started pouring from her body. This was apparently in spontaneous joy at her meeting with Babaji, who, like others in the room, reacted with childlike delight and surprise. Later, she left with her entourage, whereupon Babaji started shaking with laughter, explaining that the miracle had been effected by bags of ash under the good lady's sari, which she had activated!

Nevertheless, Babaji acknowledged that miracles do happen spontaneously through the power of God, though he strongly warned against their dangers.

"Love and devotion are the direct road to God," is what Babaji never tired of telling us, and gave a story to illustrate this.

The King and the Eight Sentries

Once two friends set out to visit their king. One arrived a little while before the other. Upon being challenged by the sentry on the outside gate, he boldly announced that he had to see the king on urgent business.

Impressed by his determination and confidence, the sentry escorted him straight through the other sentries into the king's presence. The other friend, however, was extremely nervous and unsure of himself.

'Will the king bother to see me?' he thought. 'He's so great and powerful, perhaps he will be angry.'

With these doubts and fears he approached the first guard and hesitatingly asked if it might be possible to go inside. Seeing his state of mind the sentry's mind became doubtful about this stranger. After many questions, finally he was passed through to a second sentry. Again, the same exhausting questions and then finally a third sentry. No less than eight sentries did the poor man have to pass through until at the point of utter fatigue and despondency he at last came into the presence of the king. In a kindly way the king inquired why he looked so ruffled. Whereupon the man confessed his difficulty at being admitted into his presence.

'Why didn't you just mention that you wanted to see me?' asked the king. 'You would have avoided all your difficulties. All these sentries take orders from me, as does everyone in my kingdom, so you only had to use my name and you would have been admitted directly.'

• • •

Similarly, everything in this creation belongs to God and by being His friend, we become everyone's friend. The eight sentries in the story represent the eight Siddhis or cosmic powers which guard the king, the Lord. Don't get diverted by them but go straight to God, who is the master of all. Give all your love and devotion only to Him. Once His love is won, then a man need feel no fear from his servants.

> *Even so, around Babaji, a channel for the power of God, innumerable miracles took place automatically. Some took place in the hearts and beings of people. Others were so subtle that the person concerned was hardly aware of them and others were more tangible. He never claimed responsibility for any of them.*
>
> *In 1980, when Babaji retired to a bungalow in Nasik Road, there lived in a nearby house a rickshaw driver and his wife, a simple girl who was, medically speaking, unable to conceive a child. After some years of marriage, this placed an intolerable strain on their marriage and often she would bear the marks of her husband's beatings. Finally, she swallowed her pride and approached Babaji, who reassured her.*

Don't worry, everything will be fine. You will conceive. Here, take this apple [taking an apple from the table] and eat half of it and give the other half to your husband.

> *Within a year she gave birth to a son and then, later, a daughter.*
>
> *Another dramatic intervention occurred in the Nasik bungalow one day when a desperate father begged Babaji to intercede on behalf of his daughter who had been horribly burned when her nylon sari caught fire. She was now lying in the hospital unconscious. Babaji instantly took water from the guru padukas which received daily* abhishek *and gave the water to the distraught father in a container, instructing him to pour a little into her mouth. Sure enough the girl regained consciousness and the burns healed at a phenomenal speed. Later, the girl became a regular devotee who used to attend the chanting programs.*

Evil Rebounds

Another example of the protection afforded by a jnani happened in quite a different way. A young devotee who owned a grocery shop, and who often visited Babaji, informed him that a man who had been threatening his life had himself died. Babaji remarked that this is what tends to happen with evil intention, that it rebounds on its giver. He then told the following story.

Duryodhana once approached a black magician to kill the five Pandavas. Knowing Lord Krishna himself to be a friend of the Pandavas, the magician was very reluctant. On pressure from Duryodhana, he conjured up a demon by certain rituals and told him to eat up the Pandavas.

Meanwhile, the omniscient Krishna took the five Pandavas into a forest and gave them all a small dose of poison, whereupon they all fell down like dead men. Soon the demon arrived on the scene hungry for his victims and found five apparent corpses. Furious, he returned to his creator, the magician. 'Do you expect me to eat corpses? Now I'm really hungry and will eat you.'

•　　•　　•

This is what happens to evil, so put all your faith in God. There is nothing above Him.

The ways of God are not necessarily our ways and so it is with the jnani. Established in the self beyond the pairs of opposites, his behavior often appears unpredictable and sometimes even frightening, as we can see in Babaji's gruesome story.

The Strange Ways of a Jnani

Once a certain jnani and his disciple visited a poor man's home and the jnani demanded food. In front of the man's wife and five starving children, who looked on pitifully, the jnani demanded more and more food until the meal meant for the entire family had been consumed. The disciple was quite ashamed of his guru's behavior and the last straw came when the guru took a valuable steel lota (pitcher) when the family wasn't looking and put it into his bag.

Having left the house, they passed through a field where there was a water tap. Taking the lota from his bag, the jnani filled it with water from the tap to drink. At precisely that moment, an irate farmer appeared and shouted abusively that the water was for his animals and not for the likes of him. Promptly the jnani handed the farmer the full lota and went his way. Further along the way he stopped at a dilapidated house where a man and his baby lived in a wretched condition. He again demanded food. Having finished and waiting until the man was out of sight, he seized the baby by the neck and throttled it. Then he left and went his way again.

Finally, the horrified disciple could contain himself no longer and burst out, 'Guruji, you took all the food from the first family we visited, and even stole a lota which you gave to a farmer who abused you. Now you have murdered an innocent baby. Have you gone mad?'

'Sit down here under this tree,' replied the jnani, 'and I will explain. In the first house there was so much sin weighing on the family that their situation was so desperate that there was hardly any food in the house. The food I ate and the lota I took represent that sin and I took the lot. If you return to the house you will find that the family situation has improved and the children are happy. The lota represented the sin and so I gave it to that man who was so miserly he wouldn't give a single glass of water to a thirsty man. Sin always gravitates to sin and virtue to virtue.'

The Jnani continued, 'Finally, in the last house we visited that man is my disciple and some years ago he had asked me to bless him with a son. By God's grace his wife conceived but died shortly afterward. Ever since, my disciple has been in a wretched condition. He cannot look after the child properly and both he and the child are utterly miserable. As a result he has completely neglected his remembrance of God. Consequently, not only would he not attain liberation, but both he and his child's life were in a hopeless condition.'

'This evil situation has now come to an end because by meeting his end at my hands the child will obtain a good rebirth and the man can now concentrate his life on God.'

•   •   •

Identification with the Divine Mother

In the scriptures it is said that it is out of fear of God that the wind blows. Babaji often said that fear and respect are indispensable in a seeker's relationship to his guru and to God. The fearsome aspect of the Divine Mother is represented by Kali the Destroyer depicted as having a necklace of human skulls, a sword crimson with blood and a red tongue lolling out of her mouth.

Sometimes the ways of the Divine Mother seem hard to us but look, if a child has worms in the stomach, will its mother give him sweets? No. She will prepare medicine from bitter *neem* leaves and give it to the child to cure him. If he refuses, she will have to slap him, hold his mouth open and pour in the medicine. All the worms will be expelled. Then she will take a tin full of sweets and put it in front of the child saying, 'Eat son.' The Divine Mother is like that, too, and she sometimes has to use hard methods to cure us of our faults and imperfections. Under the seeming hardness, She is all compassion and love for Her children.

Babaji was a devotee of the Mother and it was interesting to see that his mood on those days special to Her often seemed different and especially volatile. An example of his identification with the Mother can be seen from the following incident.

Once a longtime south Indian devotee visited Babaji in Nasik with his young daughter. In a mood of youthful enthusiasm the girl loudly tried to persuade an English girl who had come for Babaji's darshan to return with her and her father to visit their home. In fact, the suggestion was foolish because the house was at least fifteen miles away and disrespectful, as the English girl had come especially to visit Babaji. However, carried away by the moment, the English girl started answering the girl in a loud, excited voice about the details of returning home with them. This interchange now dominated the room, constituting disrespect for both Babaji and the assembled visitors.

Suddenly the air was rent by a terrifying roar like a lion's. The effect was devastating. Everyone's attention became riveted in astonishment and trepidation on Babaji, who was staring at the girl with protruding, rolling eyes and lolling tongue. It was as if Mother Kali herself had entered him. Then he started shouting at the girl, who, together with everyone in the room, sat transfixed and amazed. After a few seconds, Babaji returned to his normal mood as if nothing had happened. Not another word was said about the English girl's visit and father and daughter left soon afterward. Not only had the girl learned a lesson she would never forget from this bizarre episode, so had the English visitor.

A story Babaji often related illustrates the way a jnani can turn a disciple's apparently idle request or desire into a teaching situation.

Heaven and Hell

One day the disciple of a guru asked to be shown heaven. The guru agreed but only on condition that they first visited hell. Slightly disconcerted, the disciple agreed. Through the power of meditation, they traveled off in their subtle bodies. It so happened that in hell it was time for lunch and suddenly a bell rang and all the inhabitants of hell sat down in front of a magnificent feast. The only problem was that everyone had a wooden stick strapped onto both arms preventing them bending. Soon total pandemonium broke out as, with curses and shrieks of rage, the denizens of hell hurled food into the air and vainly tired to catch it in their mouths. No one got even a morsel.

With tremendous relief the disciple noticed the guru beckoning him and off they went again and after some time at last reached heaven, where, strangely enough it again happened to be lunch time. The disciple saw the same feast laid out as had been there in hell. The bell rang, soon everyone arrived for lunch, and sure enough, the same wooden pieces were fastened to both arms. Then everybody started feeding each other and there was joy and delight everywhere.

• • •

The jnani's method of teaching is, therefore, varied, sometimes humorous, sometimes even frightening, but always the subtle effect leaves its mark on the intended person.

A disciple should ask nothing from his guru except abuse as this is what kills his ego.

Often Babaji would publicly criticize and even humiliate a close disciple if he knew the person could take it, to squash their pride. If he felt a person was not strong enough to take a dressing down for a particular mistake or fault, Babaji often chastised a close disciple in the hearing of the person on that very point!

In his teaching he made, as we have seen, full use of stories from his own experience and from the scriptures such as the Ramayana and Mahabharata. His range of stories seemed practically limitless.

135

Often Babaji was also tremendously humorous in making a point.
Yet there was always a teaching hidden in it. For example, a regular
Sindhi devotee (Sind is an area in Pakistan) one day complained
bitterly about the behavior of his daughter-in-law, begging Babaji
to intervene. It seems she treated both her husband (the devotee's
son) and her in-laws with aggression and recently had beaten her
husband on the head with a shoe!

It so happened that the particular Sindhi lady in question used
to visit Babaji regularly. Coincidentally, she came the very next
day. After she had saluted Babaji and sat down, Babaji casually
addressed the assembled visitors.

Did you know that Sindhi women have a reputation for hardness
and for treating their husbands badly? Indeed, I heard recently that
some even beat their husbands over the head with shoes! Of course,
[half seriously and half humorously] women who treat their husbands like that are certainly bound for hell.

From that day there was a distinct change for the better in the
Sindhi lady. Furthermore, she suddenly started showing a special
devotion toward Babaji and began bringing him specially cooked
food! He accepted it a couple of times and then told her not to prepare
any more for him.

There are many examples of the power of Babaji's spoken word.
Once a foreign devotee was about to leave Nasik to return to his
country after a long absence. First, however, he had to make a trip
to Bombay in order to confirm his ticket. He told Babaji he thought
he might import Indian handicrafts in order to earn a living when
he got home but he had no idea how to go about it. After a moment's
thought, Babaji said: "Don't worry. You will meet someone in
Bombay to help you."

The next day the devotee arrived in Bombay and secretly
wondered what Babaji could have meant. Then, by an extraordi-
nary coincidence, he met a young man whose last business venture

136

*had just finished due to a change of government policy. He said that
exporting handicrafts would be an ideal business for him and perhaps
the two of them could be business partners. They spent the next two
days together exploring various options.*

*On his return to Nasik the foreign devotee told the story to
Babaji. 'Well,' Babaji asked, 'are you going to do it?'*

*The devotee rather sheepishly confessed that he had felt the
whole process had been rather sudden and that he was not sure if it
was wise to actually go ahead.*

*'You can lead a horse to water, but you cannot make him drink,'
was Babaji's reply.*

*But even if the disciple is fickle and confused, the jnani's love
patience, and compassion for him never wavers, even to the point of
risking his life for his disciple in the following story. It is typical of
Babaji's tongue-in-cheek humor hiding a teaching.*

Land of One Paise Per Kilo

Once a guru and his disciple visited a kingdom where everything
could be bought for one paise (a coin worth very little) per kilo! The
disciple thought he had found his heaven but his guru said he had a
bad feeling about the place and strongly advised the disciple to leave
with him immediately. Nevertheless, the disciple preferred to follow
his own will and stayed on in the land of 'one paise per kilo.'

It so happened that the king had a daughter as 'fat as a potato'
whom no one was willing to marry. So it was decreed that until
someone married his daughter, no one else in the land should marry.
Now very soon the disciple fell in love with a local girl who became
pregnant by him. What to do? At all costs, in order to save this
delicate situation, they had to get married, he decided. As soon as the
king got wind that a foreigner was defying his order, he got furious
and ordered his arrest and execution by public hanging. Immediately
soldiers erected a scaffold in the town square.

Finally, it dawned on the foolish disciple what a terrible mistake he had made in disobeying the advice of his beloved guru. Standing in front of the noose with crowds of jeering spectators, including even the king himself, he suffered intense pangs of repentance and remorse for his stupidity and infidelity. With his whole heart he prayed to his guru even as the noose was placed about his neck. Suddenly, out of nowhere, Guruji came running toward the gibbet pushing aside spectators and cursing loudly, started abusing his disciple.

'Fight me for the noose,' he whispered. Then, grabbing the noose, put it around his own neck. Whereupon the disciple shouted back and put it again on his own neck. Amazed at this spectacle, the king ordered quiet and asked, 'Old man, have you gone mad that you yourself want to be hanged?'

Guruji pleaded indignantly, 'What right has he got to win *Indra's* throne in heaven? I am his guru and I should, therefore, get the privilege!'

'What are you talking about?' cried the king.

'Look,' said Guruji, 'the man who gets hanged at this precise astrological moment is destined to win Indra's (the king of heaven) throne and that man should be me. It is my right, not his.'

'Out of the way, both of you!' yelled the king.

Leaping up and climbing onto the chair himself, he placed the noose around his own neck and kicked away the chair. Guruji and his disciple made good their escape.

•   •   •

Look at God's faithfulness and love which is always there to rescue us from our afflictions. If we truly call Him from the heart, He will save us even from the hangman's noose!

The Jnani as Giver

One tangible manifestation of Babaji's love was his habit of distributing whatever was brought to him. No one ever left him without prasad and on occasions he would give sums of money and cloth. On many occasions he himself went out to a nearby shop and bought shawls which he then gave to people. He also loved to distribute to children, sometimes clothes, sometimes watches, but above all, he loved to distribute food—sometimes succulent sweets, sometimes fruit and sometimes sugar prasad. Certainly, no one left his room empty handed. On festival days he delighted in laying on entire meals for the group of up to 75 children who attended the daily chanting program in Nasik.

One hot Sunday in April a famous artist devotee visited who had sculpted several statues for Babaji, including one of his guru, Swami Muktananda. Seeing him Babaji chuckled.

Once someone sculpted a statue of Shenni (an astrological aspect often feared to bring bad luck and disaster in its wake). Once created, the statue started dancing up and down, looking for someone to consume! So the question then arose, who would take care of this ominous aspect of men's fortunes? Of course, no one was prepared to accept the statue until someone agaram bagaram like myself volunteered! He broke the statue into small pieces and distributed them. That way no one got more than they could cope with and the burden got shared out! Similarly, whatever people bring here in the form of their sin, I distribute!

In fact, Babaji possessed an acute sense of the importance of repaying debt and not only gave freely but was very careful not to owe anything to anyone.

Even the debt incurred by accepting a single glass of milk one should not forget. In the early days in Sapta Shringh when we started

139

free food distribution to the children and offered pilgrims accommo-dation in our ashram, certain Brahmins from the village got furiously jealous that their own business monopolies were being threatened. They used to charge exorbitant fees for board and lodging from the visiting pilgrims. Under the leadership of one particular man, they even attempted to poison the food given to the children. In addition, they tried to impose a ban on anyone either visiting our ashram, working for us, or supplying anything to us. The fine for disobedi-ence was 101 rupees! At that very difficult time no one was prepared to supply us even milk, except for one poor shopkeeper who used to send milk. One should never forget such debts to others. Just a few days ago I returned from Bombay where some people gave me some money and I am thinking of giving it to him. He has seven daughters and is a poor man.

> *There are innumerable stories about Babaji's effect on people's lives and everyone in his orbit had his own story. However, he was always quick to point out that the real giver is God.*

The King and the Mahatma

Once there was a king who was in the habit of distributing gifts to his subjects, who would line up in his court to receive them. Once a certain mahatma joined the line. Arriving too late, he was told to return on the morrow. The next day the king apologized profusely for the delay and asked the mahatma to ask for what he pleased.

'First, Oh king, may I ask what you did this morning before coming here?' asked the man of God. The reply came that the king had risen, bathed and then visited the temple.

'Why?' asked the mahatma.

The king replied that he had asked God to look after his family and his kingdom and to provide a constant source of wealth in order to have enough to give his subjects every day.

'In that case,' replied the Mahatma, 'why should I take from you who are receiving from another? I can go directly to Him.'

• • •

The Jnani's Compassion

Babaji's powerful compassion and concern for others can be seen not only in his charitable work with children, but also in countless incidents throughout his life. In 1976, when Babaji lived in Sapta Shringh, a visiting Englishman got bitten on the finger by a scorpion. The pain was excruciating and he was running around the ashram crying out with the pain. Someone informed Babaji, who had retired for the night, as it was evening.

"I saw Babaji approaching me with a smile," related the Englishman afterward, "and I suddenly felt the humor of the situation and my excruciating pain became almost a joke. Babaji looked amused and took my hand and started stroking it. From that moment there was no more pain. I was entirely removed from it and was able to go to bed after an hour or so. Amazingly, I slept very well."

Once a lady, a Mexican doctor, was accompanying Babaji on an overnight train journey. Unfortunately, due to the oppressive density of passengers they became separated but finally reached their destination, Nasik. The next day the doctor told Babaji of her experience on the train. She said, "I was sitting in my compartment quite upset at the noise and confusion of the crowd. Finally, I slept and suddenly found myself sitting with Babaji, who comforted me, saying 'Don't worry, have patience.'

Babaji replied, 'I was worried about you until 12:00 p.m. and twice tried to go down the corridor but there were so many people I couldn't reach your compartment. Certainly the atma is One, so my thoughts manifested in your mind.' "

Woman, the Great Mother

Babaji's special respect for women as the visible manifestation of the Divine Mother constantly showed itself. At the time of his serious illness in 1983, a close, long-time devotee came to pay his respects. Though weak and lying on his sick bed, Babaji said immediately on seeing him:

I saw in my dream that you had a bad quarrel recently. With whom?

The devotee hung his head and said it was his wife. The man was close to tears and Babaji added:

You should never beat your wife. She is the Mother incarnate. Only because of woman do we have our bodies which were fashioned in her womb.

No matter who he may be, a person is born of woman. As a mother we take birth from her, as a child we play with her, and as a wife she grants us joy. If we are men, we should never think of ourselves as superior to her, but should treat her with great respect and care. If not, she can be the means of our downfall, just like Sita was the cause of *Ravanna's* final destruction. Jesus, Mohammed, Nityananda—all were born from a mother's womb. Therefore, we should revere women. Instead, people regard women as a means of sense pleasure and so the world sinks into a morass. Where women are revered, a country will prosper and the family where the mother is revered will be prosperous and happy. If, on the contrary, children treat their mother with lack of respect, that home will be a place of misery.

The devotee stood overcome with emotions as did the others present in the room. There were many other incidents which clearly showed Babaji's awareness of the innermost thoughts of others. On one occasion a close disciple was staying with Babaji at the Nasik bungalow over an extended period of time. One evening the young man was invited to a devotional program by members of a large ashram. During the magnificent program the young man was overwhelmed by the splendor of the singing and the large company. In his heart he longed for the excitement of a large ashram and resented the simplicity of Babaji's Nasik bungalow. Upon his return to the bungalow, it was about 10:00 p.m. and Babaji had retired for the night. However, when he opened the door he was astonished to hear Babaji shout from his room,

You can go anytime. There is no need for you to stay here if you don't want to.

The young man felt overcome with remorse and wonder. He had no feeling of being exposed, but rather he recognized a fickle aspect to his character, which had been clearly revealed by Babaji's love for him.

Another example of turning an incident into a teaching is the following. Once Babaji was sitting in the company of a number of devotees at his guru's ashram in Ganeshpuri when one of them noticed some mosquitoes feasting on Babaji's bare legs. Getting up, he tried to chase them away but Babaji used the occasion to impart a wonderful teaching on the oneness of all life and on the jnani's compassion.

Let them be. They also have to make a living and have a family to support from what they can find! See, God has given mosquitoes the means to drill for their food and how happy they are to have found it in my legs. Every creature has been given its duty by God to perform its livelihood.

143

The Sadhu and the Scorpion

Once there was a sadhu sitting beside the Ganges who noticed a scorpion drowning. In front of the astonished eyes of a passerby he reached down and picked it out of the water. The scorpion, in automatic reaction, bit him and fell back into the water. Again, the sadhu picked it up and again it bit him. The third time, however, the scorpion was safely deposited on dry land.

'Mahatmaji!' exclaimed the passerby, 'why are you saving a scorpion? In return for your kindness he is only punishing you.'

'I have my duty,' replied the sadhu, 'and he has his. My compassion for this scorpion, who, like me, is a member of the family of God's creation, forces me to react automatically in trying to save him, in spite of the cost to myself! He, on the other hand, uses the weapon that nature has given him not out of malice but because, feeling his life is threatened, he acts in the only way he knows how. In effect, he is only doing his duty in the same way as I am doing mine in saving him.'

•   •   •

A true sadhu should help others as much as he can.

> *In everything Swamiji did, love was always present and it was, perhaps, this love above everything which captured the hearts of those who came into his orbit.*

I eat love, I breathe love. God's form is love and if you want to find Him, it can only be through love. Always maintain and nurture the love that springs up from within. Don't allow it to get spoiled because when pure love gets frustrated or spoiled, it is worse than death. Love is earned by giving love. It cannot be bought. However, unlike money, the love you earn goes with you at death.

The Jnani and Death

Death is sometimes described as the great fear. It is inevitable and yet unknown. For him who is born, death is certain and for him who dies, birth is certain, says Lord Krishna in the Bhagavad Gita. Death means different things to different people. Baba Muktananda commented as follows:

For a yogi or jnani, death is not death but samadhi or liberation. For an ordinary man, death means transmigration and rebirth as a bound creature.

Babaji was constantly aware of death and always seemed almost eagerly ready for it. Indeed, he was even reluctant to accept an invitation on specific dates in the future.

When someone invites me to their house, I always reply that only if God wills it, I will come. There are no guarantees for us.

We can see a constant awareness throughout his life of the inevitability of death as well as the temporary nature of the body and the immortal essence within the individual soul which is one with the eternal principle. When death finally came to Babaji, his calm acceptance of it was, in itself, his teaching.

Even the wheat the farmer plants thinks it exists for its own sake. But no, it is the farmer who plants, waters, and harvests for **his** own sake—he has his own intentions for them.

We are like that, we think we are here for our own pleasure, but it is God who has given us life. He creates and maintains us, harvests the necessary work from us and finally destroys us. No, we are here for God's pleasure, not ours. We come into this world with our fists clenched with our karma. But when we leave it, we should go with open hands, keeping nothing.

"My soul doesn't belong to one particular place. All the three worlds are its home."

Actually we are born without caste or creed and only assume them after birth. I myself don't believe in them. Sometimes I want to remove these rudraksha beads (beads worn by seekers and Sadhus) and this orange cloth. They are like chains. I have nothing I want to do. I don't want moksha (liberation), I don't want to see God. If no one comes to me it is fine. If I have no attachment, when my time to die comes, I can go straight up. When I am free from this body, I will no longer be limited by it and will be available for all those who call me.

What difference does it make if I die in America, Australia, or India? My soul doesn't belong to one particular place. All the three worlds are its home—nether world, earth, and heaven. I belong to them all.

Epilogue

The reader may now well ask, 'Is Babaji really no more? Where is the continuation of his work?'

The answer must be, as Babaji never tired of saying, the guru principle is within, always available to us. Great souls will always be there to reveal the true path when we ourselves are ready. Therefore, in a universal sense Babaji's work continues in all places and at all times. In a more specific, localized sense, Sapta Shringh is available to all and is only a few hours journey north of Nasik (Maharashtra). Babaji's ashram stands at the foot of the towering, primordial rock of Sapta Shringh at an altitude of some 5,000 feet.

Swami Omananda (Om Baba), Babaji's nominated successor, is the spiritual head of the ashram. A powerfully built man of astonishing vitality in his late sixties, he has been a close disciple since 1955, ever since the ashram's conception. At the time of writing, he runs the ashram almost single-handedly. Under his direction the ashram has grown considerably and facilities for accommodation and welcoming visitors and pilgrims are extensive while retaining simplicity and Om Baba's distinct, personal touch.

About forty boys from humble backgrounds still receive free board and lodging in a purposely built hostel and there is an open invitation to the village children for breakfast, lunch, and evening prasad. In a sense, this is symbolic of the invitation the Divine Mother extends to all who approach Her.

The visitor finds himself easily drawn into the pristine, soaring, spiritual atmosphere created by the presence of the Divine Mother whose temple is suspended high above the ashram and by Her lovers and devotees. Babaji's Samadhi Shrine towers over where his simple kutir once stood.

It stands as an invitation and signpost that the spiritual journey and its goal is accessible to each and every one of us here and now, wherever we live and whatever our circumstances.

Encounters

Students Remember Swami Prakashananda

Peter R. Heisler, Stockbroker

Spending time with Babaji was very special. Just to be in his presence was to receive the highest teachings and blessing. All my cares and worries naturally dissolved in Babaji's presence and were replaced with a spontaneous joy, lightness, and contentment. It was as if there were a divine protection that made everything right so how could I possibly be concerned or worried about my often petty concerns.

Babaji was a selfless being who tirelessly gave and gave to those with whom he came in contact. He was like the cosmic being who took on various roles depending on the situation to serve those around him. Sometimes I witnessed him as the stern father, the guru, who needed to bring order and discipline to the situation. Other times he was the Divine Mother, tending with great care and attention to all the needs and concerns of those at hand. Other times he was the Divine Child, innocently playful and mischievous.

151

Whatever the role, to be in his presence was to be drawn into his state, the state of Divine Love where time ceases and there is only the spreading out and sharing of this love to everyone.

I remember traveling with Babaji to attend a wedding ceremony in Yeola. I was alone with him in the back seat of the taxi. At several little towns we passed on the way, we stopped and people spontaneously flocked to have his Darshan. Baba freely distributed sweets to all he met, giving ceaselessly and tirelessly from morning to night. I was struck by the fact that although I was a young, healthy man, I was exhausted that night having just gone along for the ride, whereas Babaji was fresh and still giving of himself as if he were tireless, as long as he could be of service to others.

Near the end of his life, Babaji was experiencing some health problems himself and yet still he made himself available, sharing his love and concern for others. It seemed like it should have been the other way around, with us caring for him and tending to his needs, but although we tried, it really was only Babaji taking care of us.

I remember my final darshan with him in Nasik. It was the winter just before he passed on and I had made a short visit to India. Babaji was his cheerful self inquiring about each of us. I could see that he was not well but he went out of his way to spend more time with us knowing we had made such a long journey. As my visit neared its conclusion, I felt happy and recharged under the umbrella of Babaji's love. When it was time to go, I prepared for my departure darshan and as usual, went to meet Baba in the front room which served as the satsang hall for all of us. However, this time Babaji departed from his normal procedure and instead called me back to his bedroom, especially charged with shakti, that was his private quarters (which he rarely shared with others). I was surprised and overjoyed at this great blessing. As I went to "pranam" at his feet, as I always used to do when leaving, again Babaji departed from the normal proceedings by not allowing me to "pranam" as usual, but instead looking me right in the eye, he gave me a full embrace. Once again, I felt thrilled by this unexpected turn of events and blessings. I knew there was something special about this moment, and yet I did not know why. Then Babaji looked at me again and said, "Just remember, whatever happens Babaji will always be in your heart." Then I got it, I understood the significance of this special parting. Babaji was telling me in his own way that this was the last time we would meet each other in this way. I suddenly realized that Babaji knew that he would leave his body soon and this was our final good-by. Tears rushed to my eyes and I started sobbing. Babaji only smiled with compassion. This is how I will always remember him, and yes, he is in all of our hearts. Just to remember him there is to be inspired to something greater in each one of us. What can I say but 'Thank you, thank you, thank you, for the great fortune to have met you and spent time with you, Babaji!'

• • •

Govinda Gene Gauggel, Psychotherapist

When I first arrived in Ganeshpuri, India, in 1976, I began to wonder who was a model of the ideal disciple of our Sadguru, Swami Muktananda. I found Swami Prakashananda very soon. Here was a simple, humble man whose devotion to truth and high ethics was incomparable to any others I met or watched in the presence of our guru.

I visited him often while he stayed in a room at the Ganeshpuri ashram (in Turiya Mandir). I loved his stories and kind attentiveness to each and every person who approached him. I also wondered if he had any special powers or anything that might set him apart from the rest of we ordinary humans. As I watched him over the next eight years, I could not see any quality that would set him above anyone else. I saw him express mostly love and simplicity and a conviction that God or Bhagavati (Divine Mother) was the only true Principle in operation in the universe and that we people were Her Children and that She did everything—that we do nothing. In that way he avoided assuming that he acted from any individual will. He became a living example of this, and I held him as my role model.

Once while sitting with him I told him I was in physical pain—that my whole nervous system felt painful. He responded by asking me if it was vibrations. I thought he had misunderstood (something had been lost in the translation to or from him), so I repeated myself. He asked me again, "Is it vibrations?" I sat quietly as I looked inside my body to explore my sensations as possibly being vibrations. After about twenty minutes I had no more pain. Instead of pain I began experiencing a new world of energy inside me.

He was sensitive to me and could respond to my heart. Once I had been trying to get some clarity on a personal problem and decided to visit him in order to (hopefully) get his guidance. I had to travel by bus to reach his place in Nasik Road. When I arrived he was sitting on his lawn chair on the left side of a rectangular room, next to an elaborate altar featuring icons of the Divine Mother and Baba Muktananda (and his Guru Bhagavan Nityananda). It was so colorful and attractive to the eye and warming to the heart.

After an affectionate welcome—"Ayi, ayi, Jai Jagadamba Mata Ki Jay" (Come in, come in. Victory to the Divine Mother)—he began a story. It must have been about an hour later that I realized he had addressed my concern by way of the story, and my mind was clear and happy.

I often felt that I was home in his presence, that I was complete and lacked nothing. As a small child benefits by hearing a story from his grandfather, I felt nourished and loved. I wondered what benefits could come from spending so much time listening to almost endless stories in this intimate way. I didn't think I could possibly remember most of them, to repeat to others or to distill some esoteric meaning. However, I felt something happening deep inside me as he brought his stories to life. Sometimes, lightly and humorously, he would use our names as if we were among the cast of characters! I left India feeling greatly enriched.

Later, when I returned to the U.S., I became interested in hypnotherapy, which involves the use of metaphors and short stories

154

to activate various resources within a client or to illustrate an idea. This nonconscious work could facilitate a realignment and reorganization of life experiences so that the person could function in life with more integrity. Learning this came naturally to me, having been with Babaji over a period of eight years in India. I also became aware of many unseen forces operating within me, perhaps various aspects of my personality similar to some of the characters in Babaji's stories.

He used to call me "Maharaj" (great king). He would look at me and ask "Kya ji, Maharaj," as if to ask me how I was or what was on my mind. I would usually respond, "I'm okay," while actually I was worried about something. Now I look back and think how great it would have been to tell him I was confused and worried, and to take advantage of his grace, perhaps to lighten my emotional burden.

One Christmas morning at Ganeshpuri ashram, my ex-wife and I felt a pull to go to Bombay to be with "Santa Claus." At that time Babaji was staying with a devotee to rest and to visit. So we quickly gathered our things and took the next bus to Bombay where we showed up unannounced at Mr. Daria's apartment on Malabar Hill. Sure enough Babaji was there and welcomed us with tears, saying, "You've come, you've come. Since early this morning I kept seeing your faces in my meditation. Your love is great. Now you are here. When we think of something and it comes to pass, we know it is God's will. Your love is so great." With folded hands and tears down his cheeks he looked at us with deep affection. We were speechless and very moved as we felt the sincerity of his pure heart.

Babaji was always careful to live close to his high standards of ethics. Once, several of we Westerners traveled along with him to a village near Chalisgaon. After Babaji gave darshan to many devotees, we were shown a building where we would spend the night. He had requested the men sleep outside while he and the women were to sleep inside. I got very agitated about this arrangement because my fiancee was to stay inside with him.

Soon someone came out to call me in at Babaji's request. I quickly rose and went in where I saw the women preparing their bedding on mats on the floor, while he was getting ready to sleep on his bed on one side of the room. I felt very relieved and returned to my place outside. He had been sensitive to me yet again.

Another time, my fiancee and I stopped by to see him during an ashram festival, probably Shivaratri, at his room in Turiya Mandir. We had been wondering about the impact of our getting married upon our sadhana (spiritual practices). We wanted to get his guidance on this. We were welcomed into his room as he was arranging some things in preparation for his departure the next morning. Apparently some devotees had given him packages of sev and gathiya (snacks made of chick pea flour). He placed a small square of newspaper before my fiancee and another one before me and another before himself, as we sat on the floor together.

He then took small handfuls of sev from each of several packets he had and distributed it between the three squares of newspaper. He kept taking a little from each packet and sharing it equally among the three squares until it was all distributed. As he put each handful on the paper, I felt that we were all intimately connected and that there was nothing to fear in whatever we did. It was as if he were spreading his grace among us in a ritualistic way.

As he had said so many times, "Whatever you do, you have my full blessing." After he finished this, he asked us, "Now what service can I do for you?" Nothing need be said since we felt our concern was resolved. So we said, "You have already done it."

•   •   •

Tom Stiles, Yogo Teacher

In the spring of 1982 I was at Ganeshpuri for what was to be Baba Muktananda's final birthday celebration. After eight years as a student of the meditation master, I was ready for a new point of view. I met Swami Prakashananda when Baba extended to him the rare privilege of holding Darshan for devotees. This was extremely unusual and an indication that Baba held Prakashananda to be at a high level of spiritual attainment. After Babaji's delightful storytelling and humble sharing of himself, he came out of the hall to give prasad and personal blessings. He nonchalantly sat down beside me on the couch in the adjacent hallway. He had a lapful of sugar candy which he took great delight in giving away. His ease and comfort with himself greatly appealed to me. Here was a person with whom I could be myself.

Shortly after the celebrations Gabriel Cousens and I decided to go off on a spiritual pilgrimage to several sites in the area terminating with a visit to Babaji. Upon arriving I found myself riveted, watching him. There was such love in his every movement, such a depth of peace and yet a simplicity of love he shared with us. At this time my meditation had lost its impact. I felt dry inside. I simply went through the motions of sitting and chanting and opening my heart with no result. My mind would not change states. I experienced no change in myself. I could not get inside my heart to any emotional experience. I had left Zen Buddhist meditations many years earlier for the same reason—I wanted to find my spiritual heart and a teacher with a spiritual heart. This was a central theme for me—I needed to find a way to the vastness of the spiritual realms I sensed lay within the Heart. Yet here I was after five years of a heartfelt practice without peace of mind or the feelings of connectedness that had characterized my earlier meditations. Babaji's state was in a great contrast to my own. I asked Babaji for his blessings and help in meditation. He listened attentively to my story and ended by suggesting that we both go to Trymbakeshwar. He said that this would be good for my meditation.

Trymbakeshwar is an ancient holy site, the headwaters of the Godavari River that flows nearly the width of India from west to east. It is also the samadhi site of several saints and a region surrounded by caves of yogis dug out of the cliffs near the headwaters. Gabriel and I went by taxi there and were drawn immediately to the central towering temple known as one of twelve special jyotilingams. These are temples that have an invisible lingam (male phallic symbol) arising as a pillar of light from the spring of a yoni (female genital) stone. In this case the central sanctum sanctorum was a place in which a milk white water flowed from the yoni. I found myself soon contemplating this jyotilingam as we made our way to the central space under the high dome of the temple. The floor was carved with an enormous turtle. We sat there as I deepened my contemplation of what is the nature of the jyotilingam? I felt Prakashananda's presence deeply embedded within me respond. There was a sense that he was answering my questions and also blessing me with a vision of the nature of the lingam. I felt his presence opening my chest as if there were a shirt there. As the two sides of my chest split I saw the head of Shiva as my own chest. My own head became the many heads of a cobra showering a protective grace-filled light onto the Shiva that was my chest. Then I experienced an incredible ecstasy of light filling my body showering me from the inside. The lingam of my body became a wand of light. The brilliance of that light was like an arc welder, intense to look at yet captivating and not overpowering. I felt a tremendous wave of bliss flood my being and hot tears traced their way down my face. My Heart, like a dam, had burst and overflowed through my eyes. I had found the Heart I had been looking for all those many years. I felt all this as a direct result of being with Babaji. The whole experience of having a Heart overflowing with grace I experienced as a blessing from him.

Upon returning to Nasik Road I found that my previously dry state of meditation completely changed and I found myself once again spiritually alive. Just being in Babaji's presence was a blessing to me. I found that watching him or just simply being with him gave me great peace. He was truly a person that put me at tremendous ease. Yet I found myself thinking that this is such a simple thing and yet it is also quite profound. I kept finding myself asking—Who is he? What is he all about?

One night while massaging his legs he allowed me to continue and do his whole body. When I got to his belly this question began to burn inside my mind. Who is he? Who am I? While holding these questions inside myself, I gently pushed on his belly. The answer came that his body was like a water bed. When I pushed on one side a ripple would go effortlessly through his entire body and then ripple back to me with the same force. I asked myself, What is he made of? What is this body? I closed my eyes and I saw a beautiful effulgent blue like the ocean shimmering in the morning light. As I continued to look the blue spread to the horizon and beyond to encompass the sky, I could not distinguish air from water. All elements of his body and of my perception were the same glimmering blue. I had an image of a million tiny lights within the blue field all shining continuously. My eyes began to water with warm tears of joy and great love as I felt his belly. Then I opened my eyes and looked at his body and he simply smiled at me. One of those all knowing smiles that allowed me to just be my Self. Just enjoying the joy that was his body while serving him through the act of giving a massage. There was no feeling of him giving me energy or vice versa. There was a natural acceptance of each other's role in life in this moment just being together. In that moment there was a grace that has never left me, a memory that continues to live on and on, vividly, as a connection to my spiritual Heart.

•   •   •

Pierre Pulling, Carpenter

A simply garbed sadhu entered the temple and turned toward the shrine. Many of the Indians inside stood up and took turns bowing before this unassuming monk, pressing their fingers and foreheads upon his sturdy feet. As a result, he could not proceed forward. Yet the swami did not lose his focus of offering his respects to the deity of the temple as he folded his hands before his heart to honor each person who blocked his path. Someone whispered to me, 'He is an enlightened being.'

I had met Swami Prakashananda! Never had I seen patience and dignity expressed so naturally and so warmly. Graciousness of this breadth and depth seemed light years removed from my own experiences and expectations of who I might become. Little did I imagine that some day this humble man would also draw my tired heart before him in order to offer me that 'water of eternal life drinking which one never thirsts again.'

Ten years later I had an opportunity to spend time in India with Swami Prakashananda. Swamiji welcomed me with a hearty "Amba Mata Ki Jaya! Sadgurunath Maharaj Ki Jaya!" (Victory to the Divine Mother! Victory to the true guru, Lord and great king!) He inquired affectionately about my family and I relaxed in his satsang room as he greeted other visitors with the same two phrases. How glad of heart we were to hear that friendly greeting—resounding with the surety of deep experience.

It is eight years now, since we were privileged to see his face or write him a letter. Yet the fullness of his voice still booms in my ear and memories: a joy which conquers the boundaries of mind, time, and place. His words still ring more vividly than the noise of traffic on the streets outside: "You take everything you want from the earth, your Mother. Then you trample her, pollute her, and defecate upon her. How does she respond? In return, she forgives you; she sends up lush vegetation to feed, nourish, and clothe you. She mends your desecrations with verdant aromatic growth. She longs to

160

beautify your life. She always wishes for you the best of creation and the warmth of love and tenderness. These qualities are the foundation of all hearts but are especially given to women."

Again and again Swami Prakashananda would gently remind me to see life with a greater awareness of the Mother. "In India we always say the woman's name first, even among the gods: 'Sita-Ram, Radhe-Shyam, Lakshmi-Narayan, Uma-Maheshwar.' Why? Why is the husband secondary? Because mankind will never attain happiness and peace if we neglect to honor and cherish women."

It has taken me time to imbibe these words, for the contrary tendencies to 'pillage and lay waste' seem deeply rooted in the psyche. But the words of a guru have mysterious power. Many years later they continue to act both in the subconscious mind and outside: creating 'coincidental' opportunities for growth and changes. At the time, however, I had no concern for future results. My only interest was to remain absorbed in those amazing graces which unfolded before the mischievous smiles of our 'agaram bagaram baba.' Somehow in his presence my limitations were not inadequacies—quite in contrast to life out in the world.

We were a motley bunch gathering around our swami in those days, from many countries and backgrounds. The fact of Babaji's failing health urged me to make the journey and to return again the following years, despite the many difficulties of so much travel. What kind destiny brought me to sit in the cocoon of his parlor, softly overwhelmed by waves of his tender care? I was, at best, a second-rate actor in the great puppet show of life. What prayers or kindness had *I* ever done to deserve such good fortune? But did I have any inkling that these sacred gifts would soon become my challenges?

This story of a man who belonged utterly to the Mother became a song of gladness in the lives of those who met him. He brought Her love and laughter into many, many hearts with an ease and a surety that has, in my case, given life a freshness and preciousness which was missing before.

Thanks to this book the priceless gifts of compassion flowing through our 'agaram bagaram baba' can continue to roll on, embracing and refreshing many lives. This is the story of a man who belongs so completely to the Divine Mother that he easily brought Her love and laughter into many hearts. Now many more will be refreshed with Swami Prakashananda's warm welcome: "Amba Mata ki jaya! Sadgurunath maharaj ki jaya!"

•   •   •

Marjorie

Being raised in this lifetime as a "Jewish American Princess" and made to feel special, had been a difficult part to play. Underneath that part were insecurities and no clue of who I was and what the meaning of living was all about.

My first experience of Babaji was in Ganeshpuri, India at Swami Muktananda's ashram in May 1982. Babaji would meet people and tell folklore stories that conveyed deep meaning. These stories addressed issues that we all needed to take a look at in our lives. I remember sitting there in awe of his joy, his sincerity, and his love. At last my heart was in a safe place and I felt it burst open and I wept. I found that I wanted to sit with him at every free moment and so when it was time for Babaji to return to his home in Nasik, I requested to come and stay with him. He consented and over the next five years I spent a total of two and a half years with him.

Swami Prakashananda showed me that it was possible to live in the world, keep to a spiritual mood of unconditional love, service, and surrender to the Divine Mother's will, under any circumstance and situation that arose. Babaji was an example of a whole human being living his everyday life.

Observing the day to day life around him, it seemed as if there were nothing extraordinary going on. Babaji met with many people

162

on a daily basis who came to him with all sorts of concerns and issues. The discussions throughout the day ranged from politics to relationships, from advice on business to food recipes, from deep spiritual knowledge to the weather or health issues. Love permeated the atmosphere around him and contact with him brought peace to the mind and uplifted the heart. I have never met anyone who had such complete patience, integrity, and unconditional love.

My experience of living with Swami Prakashananda was of the unitive experience of God occurring in everyday life. There were so many subtle experiences and unfoldings that occurred during my time spent with him that it is hard to describe. This process is still unfolding as I write at this moment!

The most important teachings that I came away with are that I am a lovable human being and that the answers to my questions and the key to my search for peace are right within my own being. Babaji allowed me to empower myself. He constantly showered me with love, patience, wisdom, and spiritual energy. I could not take as much as he gave, but I took what I was capable of holding and, as I mentioned, it keeps unfolding. Life is an ongoing exciting process. Babaji healed me through love and I feel that love is the greatest healer of all.

• • •

Glossary

Abhishek—*a ritualistic pouring of water on the statue or representation of a deity.*
Adivasi—*literarily, 'original people.'*
Angustha Purusha—*the thumb-sized individual soul in the heart.*
Anna—*a small denomination of money.*
Anustan—*a ritual penance.*
Asan—*a piece of wool or other material used to sit on in meditation; a hatha yoga posture.*
Atma Jnan—*knowledge of the Supreme Self.*
Atma Jyoti—*the light of the soul.*
Atman/Atma—*atman is usually used to mean universal consciousness, whereas atma is atman manifested in the individual.*
Baba/Babaji—*literally, father; "-ji" is added to indicate respect.*
Bal Bhojan—*free food made available for children.*
Bhagavati—*the Divine Mother.*
Bhagwan—*a title given to God; Lord.*

Bhajan—*usually means group chanting with musical instruments.*
Bhagavati—*the dynamic aspect of God; Divine Mother.*
Bindu—*literally point; the blue bindu is seen in the final stages of meditation.*
Bramachari—*a celibate seeker.*
Brahman—*Universal Consciousness, the Absolute.*
Brahmin—*a priest, member of priestly caste.*
Congress Party—*the political party first led by Mahatma Gandhi which ruled India after Independence in 1948.*
Dakshina—*money or offering made to a deity or saint.*
Darshan—*sight of a deity or saint.*
Dharma—*righteousness, duty.*
Dattatreya—*a divine personality embodying Brahma, Vishnu, and Shiva.*
Devi—*the divine power.*
Dharmasala—*a resting place for pilgrims.*
Dhoti—*a cloth worn in North India similar to trousers.*
Diksha—*spiritual initiation.*
Durgah—*tomb of a muslim saint.*
Duryodhana—*the king in the epic* Mahabharata *whose misguidedness caused an appalling war.*
Gadi—*the seat of authority of a spiritual lineage or ashram.*
Ganesha—*son of Lord Shiva and remover of obstacles in Hindu cosmology.*
Ghat—*the steps leading down to a bathing area on a river.*
Ghee—*clarified butter*
Gurugita—*a hymn to the Guru originating from the Skanda Purana, a Hindu scripture.*
Gurukrula—*the vedic system of education based on the guru-disciple relationship.*
Guru Tattva—*The guru principle that leads a seeker back to God.*
Hari—*God as preserver (Vishnu).*
Hanuman—*the monkey hero of the epic* Ramayana.
Indra—*king of heaven in Hindu cosmology.*

166

Ishta Devata—*the particular deity of an individual or family.*
Jagadamba—*the divine world Mother, Shakti.*
Jal Samadhi—*upon death the body of a saint is offered to the waters of a sacred river.*
Janaka—*a king and enlightened jnani; father of Sita.*
Japa—*recitation of mantra(s).*
Jivatma/Jiva—*individual soul.*
Jnani—*a knower of the truth.*
Jnan—*spiritual knowledge.*
Kailas—*a mountain in Tibet which is also traditionally the abode of Lord Shiva.*
Kailas Math—*the monastery in Nasik of the Saraswati order of monks.*
Kali–*the Divine Mother in Her fearsome aspect.*
Kali Yuga—*the present age in which unrighteousness prevails.*
Karma—*store of past actions accumulated by the soul.*
Kaveri—*a large river in South India.*
Khichari—*a dish or rice and pulses.*
Kum Kum—*a red powder applied on the forehead and feet of individuals and deities during worship.*
Kumbak—*spontaneous yogic retention of the breath.*
Kundalini—*the dynamic aspect of universal consciousness when it resides in a human being, dwelling at the base of the spine.*
Kutir—*hut*
Ladoo—*an Indian sweet in the form of a ball.*
Langhoti—*a loin cloth.*
Laxman—*brother of Lord Rama.*
Laxmi—*Shakti in her aspect of wealth, beauty, and bounty; wife of Vishnu.*
Leela—*the unfolding, cosmic drama or sport of the divine power.*
Lingam—*representation in stone of the Absolute, worshipped throughout India.*
Lota—*a drinking vessel.*
Lungi—*a cloth like a skirt worn by men, especially in South India.*
Madrasi—*a person from Madras.*

Mahabharata—*an epic poem culminating in a stupendous battle; scene of the "Bhagavad Gita."*
Mahamandelshwar—*the spiritual head of an order of monks.*
Mahapurusha—*a highly evolved being.*
Maharaj—*literally great king; a title of respect often given to a saint.*
Mahasamadhi—*the process whereby a great being consciously leaves the body at the time of death.*
Mahatma—*a great soul.*
Mahut—*an elephant keeper.*
Manasaror—*a lake near Kailas, also an object of pilgrimage.*
Mantra—*a Sanskrit invocation used in meditation.*
Meenakshi—*the temple of the Divine Mother at Madurai, South India.*
Moksha—*freedom from identification with phenomenal existence.*
Muktananda Swami (Baba)—*a Siddha guru who visited the West awakening thousands of seekers through shaktipat; Babaji's guru who took mahasamadhi in 1982.*
Nada—*sound aspect of universal consciousness heard in meditation.*
Nas Sampradaya—*literally "nose lineage."*
Nauchandi Yajna—*an elaborate fire sacrifice performed in honor of the Divine Mother.*
Nandi Mandap—*the area in a shiva temple sacred to Nandi, the bull of Lord Shiva.*
Neem—*trees whose leaves are bitter, and yet medicinal.*
Nityananda—*a great saint and guru of Swami Muktananda.*
Padukas—*wooden sandals representing the guru and his blessing.*
Palki—*a special litter carried by four bearers on which a representation of the Divine is carried.*
Pandas—*priests.*
Pandavas—*the five brothers, heroes featured in the epic* Mahabharata, *who include Yudhisthira and Arjuna.*
Pandharapur—*the pilgrimage center of devotion to Krishna in the form of Lord Vithal in Maharashtra.*
Parvati—*consort of Lord Shiva.*
Pradakshina—*the circumambulation of a deity done as an act of worship.*

Prasad—*consecrated food.*
Puja—*ritual worship; a small altar.*
Punya—*merit derived from virtuous actions.*
Rama—*Avatar (human embodiment) of Vishnu in the epic* Ramayana; *husband of Sita.*
Ravana—*the demon king who abducted Sita, Rama's wife, in the epic* Ramayana.
Sadhak—*a seeker of truth.*
Sadhana—*spiritual practices.*
Sadhu—*a renunciant.*
Sadguru—*true guru.*
Sahasrar—*spiritual center in the head.*
Samadhi—*superconscious state of meditation; burial place of a saint.*
Samsar—*phenomenal existence.*
Sanyas—*monkhood; renunciation.*
Sanyassi—*monk, renunciant.*
Satyagraha—*Mahatma Gandhi's movement of peaceful non-cooperation with the British rulers prior to India's independence.*
Satyagri—*a non-cooperator in Ghandi's Independence Movement.*
Satpurusha—*a great being, mahatma.*
Shakti—*the dynamic aspect of universal consciousness.*
Shaktipat—*transmission of the guru's spiritual energy to the disciple.*
Shakti Peeth—*a place where the Divine power is especially manifest.*
Shastras—*scriptures.*
Shiva—*God in His aspect of dissolution. Consort of Shakti. Often used to signify the absolute. Often depicted as an ascetic with matted locks.*
Shriyantra—*a geometrical design representing the Devi.*
Siddha—*perfected being.*
Siddha Vidya/Yoga—*the yoga activated by the awakened kundalini.*
Siddhi (Prapti)—*siddhis are powers; siddhiprapti means their attainment.*
Sita—*the wife of Lord Rama.*
Skanda Purana—*a scripture in which the Gurugita occurs.*
Tapasya (Tapas)—*intense austerities undergone in order to attain spiritual fruitage.*

Tiffin Carrier—*a stainless steel food container.*
Vaikuntha—*Vishnu's heaven in Hindu cosmology.*
Vijnan—*Spiritual knowledge.*
Vishnu—*the second member of the Hindu trinity; the sustainer; the husband of Laxmi.*
Wallah—*colloquialism for person.*
Western Ghats—*range of mountains upon which Sapta Shringh is situated.*
Upadesh—*spiritual instruction.*
Yagna—*a ritual fire sacrifice.*
Yudhisthira—*the eldest of the five pandavas who play a major role in the epic "Mahabharata." He is often regarded as the epitomy of righteous behavior.*
Zilla—*area.*

Index

About the Author

The son of a British diplomat, Titus Foster spent much of his early years in various countries of the world. Born in Vienna, he was educated in Poland, South Africa, and England.

In 1976, he met Swami Prakashananda near Bombay, India. Titus lived in his close company for eight years as a *chela* (disciple). Titus' years with Prakashananda radically changed his outlook and under-standing. Under Swamiji's guidance he underwent a profound spiritual transformation and was extraordinarily fortunate to be treated as his spiritual son.

Titus immersed himself in Indian culture and spirituality and learned to speak Hindi. Most of all, he was privileged to share and participate in the unique atmosphere and viewpoint of a self-realized being. Profoundly affected by his contact with Swamiji, Titus noted down various incidents, anecdotes, and teachings, which later became this book.

Upon his return to England in 1987, Titus seriously considered a vocation as a Christian monk but destiny decided otherwise. He now lives in Sussex, England with his wife and two children and practices acupuncture and complementary medicine.